WILLHOITE'S HOLLYWOOD

Willhoite's Hollywood

CARICATURES BY
MICHAEL WILLHOITE

BOSTON: ALYSON PUBLICATIONS, INC.

Copyright © 1994 by Michael Willhoite. All rights reserved.
Book design by Michael Willhoite.

Typeset and printed in the United States of America.

Published by Alyson Publications, Inc.,
40 Plympton Street, Boston, Massachusetts 02118.

First edition: December 1994

2 4 5 3 1

ISBN 1-55583-272-5

THE CAST (In order of appearance)

INTRODUCTION : 7

Peter Lorre : 10
Cesar Romero : 11
Barbara Stanwyck : 12
Robert Taylor : 13
Joan Crawford : 14
James Bridges : 15
Tommy Kirk : 16
David Geffen : 17
Marlene Dietrich : 18
Raymond Burr : 19
Cecil Beaton : 20
Hattie McDaniel : 21
Ricky Nelson : 22
John Gielgud : 23
John Waters : 24
Gertrude Lawrence : 25
Sal Mineo : 26
Tyrone Power : 27
Clifton Webb : 28
Montgomery Clift : 29
Michael Redgrave : 30
Dorothy Arzner : 31
Billy De Wolfe : 32
Divine : 33
Emlyn Williams : 34
Rock Hudson : 35
Will Geer : 36
Harvey Fierstein : 37
Alla Nazimova : 38
Luchino Visconti : 39

Paul Lynde : 40
F.W. Murnau : 41
John Garfield : 42
Franklin Pangborn : 43
Janet Gaynor : 44
John Schlesinger : 45
Simon Callow : 46
Ian Charleson : 47
Howard Hughes : 48
Agnes Moorehead : 49
James Whale : 50
Edmund Goulding : 51
Kay Thompson : 52
Wayland Flowers : 53
Dolores Del Rio : 54
Cedric Gibbons : 55
Dan Dailey : 56
Beatrice Lillie : 57
Ramon Novarro : 58
Albert Dekker : 59
Louise Brooks : 60
Rod La Rocque : 61
Franco Zeffirelli : 62
Marlon Brando : 63
Judy Holliday : 64
Jack Buchanan : 65
David Cassidy : 66
Nelson Eddy : 67
Rudolph Valentino : 68
Natasha Rambova : 69

Danny Kaye : 70
George Nader : 71
Vincente Minnelli : 72
Judy Garland : 73
Liza Minnelli : 74
William Desmond Taylor : 75
Greta Garbo : 76
Mauritz Stiller : 77
Clark Gable : 78
Monty Woolley : 79
Charles Laughton : 80
Edward Everett Horton : 81
Cary Grant : 82
Randolph Scott : 83
Colin Higgins : 84
Ethel Waters : 85
Jack Cassidy : 86
Leonard Frey : 87
Howard Ashman : 88
Conrad Veidt : 89
Paulette Goddard : 90
Ernest Thesiger : 91
H.B. Warner : 92
Richard Burton : 93
Rudy Vallee : 94
Michael Jackson : 95
Cole Porter : 96
George Cukor : 97
Bette Davis : 98
Roger Edens : 99

Richard Deacon : 100
Peter Lawford : 101
Tom Hulce : 102
Craig Russell : 103
Tony Richardson : 104
Laurence Olivier : 105
Van Johnson : 106
Marilyn Monroe : 107
Jim Nabors : 108
Oliver Stone : 109
Michael Jeter : 110
Lily Tomlin : 111

Laurence Harvey : 112
William Haines : 113
James Dean : 114
Charles Walters : 115
Sandra Bernhard : 116
Errol Flynn : 117
Anthony Perkins : 118
Nick Adams : 119
Judy Carne : 120
Dick Sargent : 121
James Ivory : 122
Ismail Merchant : 123

Max Adrian : 124
Mitchell Leisen : 125
Hanif Kureishi : 126
Sheila James Kuehl : 127
Robert Morse : 128
Edith Head : 129
Maria Schneider : 130
Tab Hunter : 131
Charles Nelson Reilly : 132
Tommy Tune : 133
Casey Donovan : 134
Carole Landis : 135

INTRODUCTION

Over the last dozen years my caricatures for the *Washington Blade* have included a large number of actors. While the book before you is a modest valentine to gay men and lesbians in show business, it's also a tribute to moviemaking itself, the premiere art of the twentieth century. I cover television and pop music as well, but my main focus is the Hollywood of the film industry. I've included several foreign stars and directors in the book, too, because Hollywood is far larger than the modest parcel of land nestled among the suburbs of greater Los Angeles. Even now, when most of the celebrated studios have been broken up and the future more than likely belongs to the film-school whiz kids and independents, this glamorous, legendary Hollywood is still vividly alive to me. Alas, the agents, the moneymen, the deal makers own the town now — as they always did. Still, the heart and soul of Hollywood belongs to those of us who believe in magic. Yeah, I know that's a cliché, but an ardent lover can perhaps be forgiven for stating the obvious.

A brief browse through this book will reveal that I love, even venerate movies. *All* movies: primitive flickers from the earliest days of the silents, movies from the great golden age between the wars, movies made last week. Foreign films, good films, bad films — I love the whole damn show, but I have a special affection for musicals, *film noir*, screwball comedies, and the glossy studio product exemplified by MGM in its platinum period. When asked my favorite picture, I usually say $8\frac{1}{2}$ or *Citizen Kane*, and I mean it at the time, but I suppose the most resonant movie of all to me is *The Wizard of Oz*. I wish I could reasonably explain why it fills me with wonder to this day, after countless viewings. But I can't. It's obviously a touchstone for millions of gay men and probably women too. But the reason is certainly significant beyond the fact that it stars Judy Garland, and so far nobody has explained to my satisfaction exactly why it means so much to us.

Really, what *is* it about gay men and the movies? Long before I had reached the age of sexual self-discovery, I sensed a special bond between that little boy from Hobart, Oklahoma, and the orange blossom–scented Valhalla on the West Coast. Hollywood was barely real to me, but I yearned for it as I sat there in the Esquire Theater, waiting for the actors to come flickering forth out of the darkness.

Ahhh, the actors. I loved them all, even (God forgive me) Jerry Lewis. But strangely enough, when I remember the movies of my childhood, the 1950s, the first figure to come to mind is Randolph Scott, the leathery, very minor star of so many program westerns. He was in so many of those Saturday afternoon movies then. It's right and strangely comforting that he should appear in my book.

Adulthood intensified my love of film. *Bonnie and Clyde* was the great eye-opener, almost an epiphany. Watching Warren Beatty and Faye Dunaway jerking through their final dance of death, I saw film for the first time as *art*. My interest in directors grew rapidly. Hitchcock, Billy Wilder, Orson Welles, John Huston: these men became as potent in my imagination as any of the great actors. Hollywood itself became more real, and among my most cherished movies are a handful that hold the mirror to Hollywood's own face: *The Bad and the Beautiful, A Star Is Born, Singin' in the Rain.*

And *Sunset Boulevard*. No other movie I can think of so perfectly embodies the dream of Hollywood in collision with its sometimes sordid reality. Wilder's brilliantly mordant satire is the truest picture *ever* of the film capital. It's Hollywood caught in the most pitiless light. Yet its magic still holds. I'm afraid I can never fully enjoy the musical *Sunset Boulevard*, a humdrum, slavish adaptation that completely misses the movie's true essence, its black humor.

Because I've been doing these drawings for so long, many of my friends come to me as the oracle, the one who *knows* who's gay in Hollywood and who is not. Still, I only know what I've been told, or have read. Of course, everyone hears rumors, and many assume I can give them the straight scoop (as it were). Sometimes I can. But I've lost count of how many of my friends, straight ones generally, have come up to me with an avid look and asked breathlessly, "Is Richard Gere gay? Is Jodie Foster? Is *Lassie?*"

A couple of these people may be straight, after all. Liza Minnelli certainly is, but she is here by grace of being one of the most beloved of gay icons, as is Bette Davis. Joan Crawford's lesbianism remains a matter of conjecture, but what the hell, here she is. Some, *many*, of course remain in the closet, and so must go unrecorded here. Oh, if *only* I could draw that star of a great sixties sitcom, or that musical comedy goddess I've admired for years!

It's a pleasure to express my thanks again to Sasha Alyson and to Don Michaels of the *Washington Blade,* where most of these drawings first appeared. My friend Kippy Goldfarb (a superb actress, by the way) took the witty jacket photo.

Ever since I started doing these drawings for the *Blade* I've had my antennae out for any tidbits I could use. Luckily, I'm an omnivorous reader, especially on film lore. I got oodles of wicked gossip from Kenneth Anger's *Hollywood Babylon* and its sequel, two of the most delectably mean-spirited and irresistible books ever written on the movies. A couple of bite-sized tidbits came from Boze Hadleigh's delightful dishfest *Hollywood Babble On.* My most valuable research tool was *The Film Encyclopedia*, by the late Ephraim Katz, from which I got so much sheer information. It's impossible to overestimate the value of this magisterial volume. It's scholarly, it's accurate, *and* it's entertaining, easily the best film reference book in print, probably the best ever written.

But he can't tell you about Lassie either.

To Janet,
my baby sister — and my first friend

In *M*, Peter Lorre's first sound film, he played a child murderer, parsnip-pale, with huge, hot black eyes. But by the end of the film his wizardry has actually aroused the audience's *sympathy* for this psychopathic monster, as he's pursued by the brutish mob, a terrified animal. Ah, those eyes, those huge, vulnerable, eyes. They could flash from sinister to sympathetic in a twinkling, and kept him working steadily. (Thirty-four films in the forties alone, including such immortals as *The Maltese Falcon* and *Casablanca*.) In the thirties, this tiny Hungarian was sleek Mr. Moto in a series of programmers. But as he ballooned up (and down and up again) he played a kaleidoscope of character roles, usually foreigners — even a bubbly Russian commissar in the musical *Silk Stockings*.

Cesar Romero was a tall, suave, *very* single Latin-lover type, a former ballroom dancer who made scores of fine movies. Except for the *Cisco Kid* series he was rarely the leading man. (Did the 1940 title *The Gay Caballero* make him a teensy bit edgy?) "Confirmed bachelor" was generally accepted Hollywoodese for "raving queen — next topic please." But when pressed by the tactless or hopelessly naive, he declared that, alas, he could never marry, because, er, the poor girl would have to, uh, cope with his large closeknit family and (cough), er, *you* know ... So he remained invaluable as an extra man at Hollywood dinner parties. And employed. Romero had a sly gift for comedy, which he *reveled* in when he played the Joker in the TV series *Batman*.

Ruby Stevens, ex-chorine, should never have changed her name to Barbara Stanwyck. Ruby Stevens *fit* better. At bottom she remained a take-charge dame from Brooklyn, *whatever* role she attempted. Comedy, drama, even westerns — she could do it all. Only Bette Davis had a greater range. Stanwyck was supreme in screwball comedy, easily the equal of Hepburn or Jean Arthur *(Ball of Fire, The Lady Eve)*. But corrupting Fred MacMurray in *Double Indemnity* (above), Stanwyck could out-*fatale* any *femme* in the business. Director Cecil B. DeMille cited her as his favorite actress, the total pro. "I've never worked with an actress more cooperative, less temperamental, a better workman." Married (briefly) to Broadway's Frank Fay and even longer to Robert Taylor, she was still one of our own.

Robert Taylor: hardly a glamorous *nom de cinéma*, right? But as Spangler Arlington Brugh he would have been hooted off the screen. In *Camille*, Taylor's Armand was almost prettier than Garbo. *Lovely*, really. MGM didn't help matters much either, by billing him as "The Man with the Perfect Profile." But with hard work in lieu of talent, he soldiered on. (Eventually, the beauty developed hard edges, too.) He even played the game by marrying a couple of times. His reward was a steady if unspectacular career. There *was* one tiny hitch. When Sen. Joseph McCarthy turned his malignant gaze on the film industry, Taylor was called as a witness. Well, it was not a pretty time — and Taylor's testimony wasn't a pretty sight: he sang like a canary.

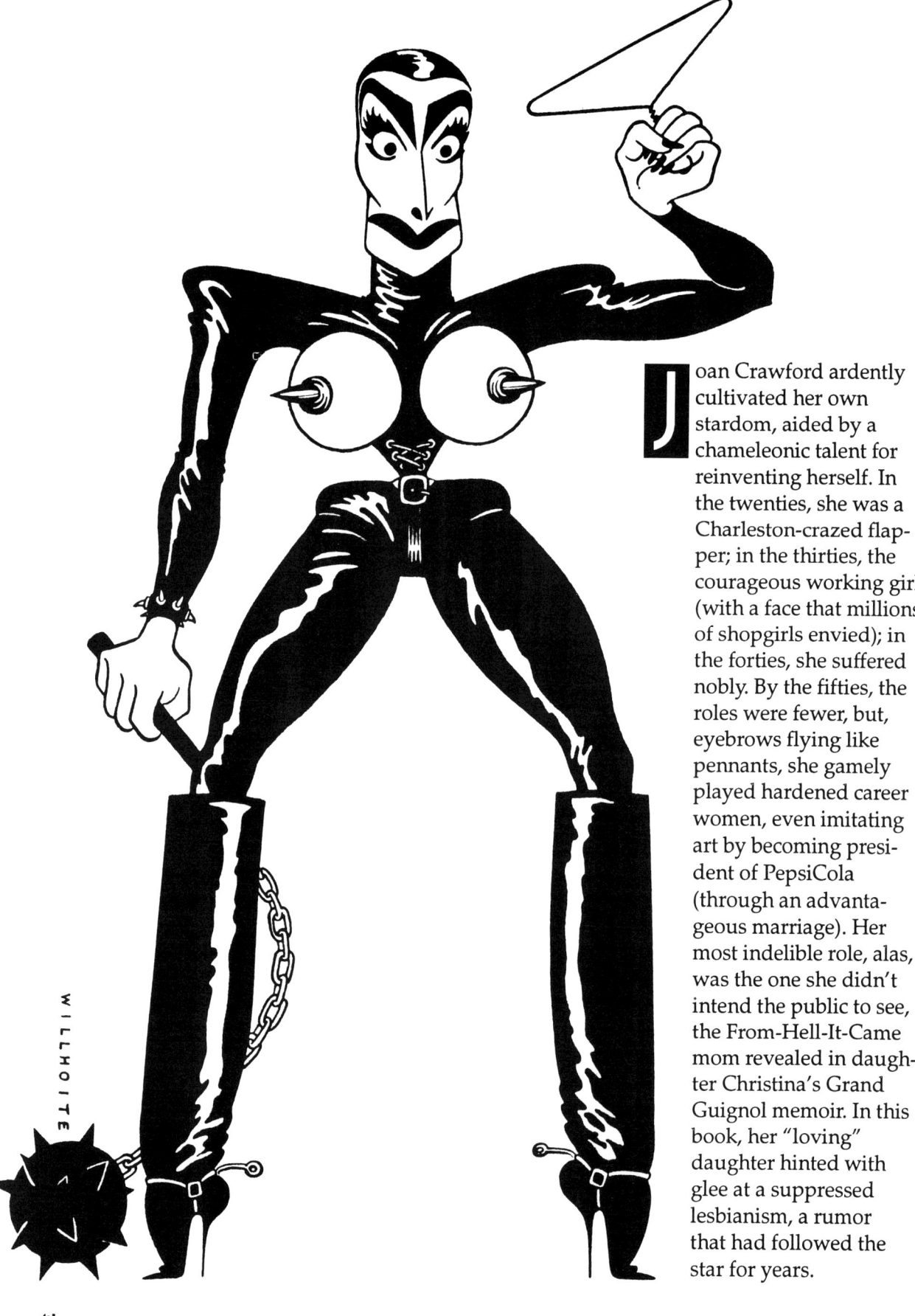

Joan Crawford ardently cultivated her own stardom, aided by a chameleonic talent for reinventing herself. In the twenties, she was a Charleston-crazed flapper; in the thirties, the courageous working girl (with a face that millions of shopgirls envied); in the forties, she suffered nobly. By the fifties, the roles were fewer, but, eyebrows flying like pennants, she gamely played hardened career women, even imitating art by becoming president of PepsiCola (through an advantageous marriage). Her most indelible role, alas, was the one she didn't intend the public to see, the From-Hell-It-Came mom revealed in daughter Christina's Grand Guignol memoir. In this book, her "loving" daughter hinted with glee at a suppressed lesbianism, a rumor that had followed the star for years.

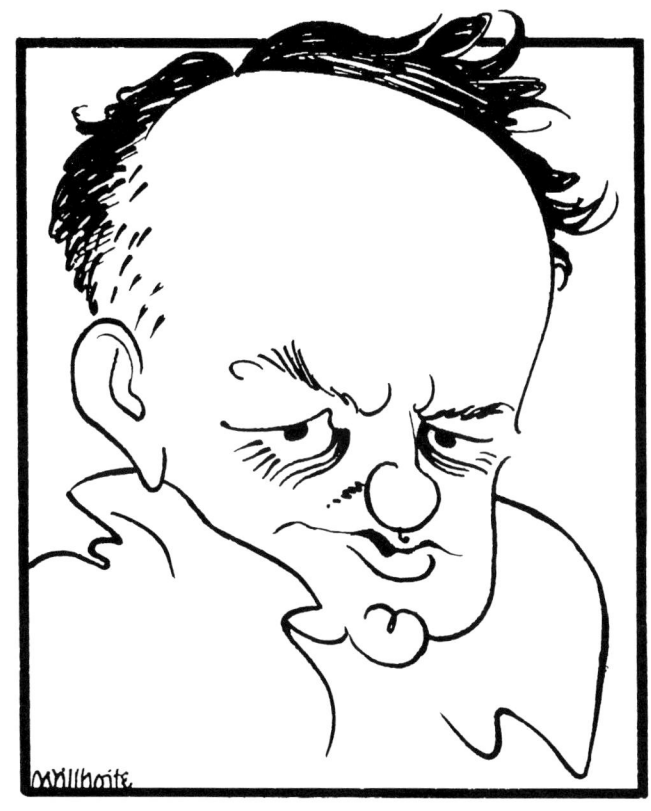

The late James Bridges started as an actor. He first lay siege to the stage, then television (over fifty programs), then movies like *Johnny Trouble* and *Faces*. But acting eventually fell by the wayside: he wanted to write and direct. An early script, *The Appaloosa*, got his foot in the door. The first of his scripts he directed was *The Baby Maker*, a dippy potboiler. Next came *September 30, 1955*, which addressed the mystique of James Dean, and the way American youth reacted to his death. He hit his stride with *The Paper Chase*, but struck gold with *The China Syndrome*, when the Three Mile Island disaster made the movie uncomfortably relevant. And a fine career was on its way. His life-partner was Jack Larson — yes, folks, *Superman*'s Jimmy Olsen.

It took some of us years to forgive Tommy Kirk for shooting *Old Yeller*. But hey, someone had to do it, right? At least he made up for it by *becoming* a dog in his next movie. Kirk was one of Disney's busiest young actors. But like most of them in that innocent time he was used indiscriminately, thrown willy-nilly into puerile "adventure" flicks, sexless Fred MacMurray comedies, and beach movies. And the ultimate horror — *Babes in Toyland*. While Annette Funicello, Tommy Sands, and the president of the Ray Bolger Fan Club strove to out-cute each other, Kirk smoothly walked off with the movie, virtually the only good thing in it. So. Why on earth did this resourceful comic actor retire from showbiz? Come back, Tommy.

Here's the man who *owns* show business. A colossus among producers, megamillionaire David Geffen is one of the most powerful princes of the entertainment world. Geffen started out as a poor boy from Brooklyn. He scaled Parnassus as a crackerjack young agent, and swiftly moved into producing records. The first movie he produced was the respectable flop *Personal Best*, but *Beetlejuice* put him in the winners' column. He even ventures into the shark-infested waters of Broadway. His enemies (and yes, he has *armies* of them) must have rejoiced when he backed Sondheim's superb off-Broadway musical *Assassins* and rather took a bath. He probably didn't even notice the loss. Geffen recently came out of the closet. Let's just hope he makes the time to *enjoy* it a little.

marlene Dietrich was a cool customer, the wittiest, most persuasive vamp of the sound era. Watch her in *Desire,* toying with Gary Cooper as a cat plays with a mouse, or her sly, half-adversarial mating dance with Jimmy Stewart in *Destry Rides Again.* Her tools were simple: a sinuous body, a singing voice that set the juices flowing, and an ironic wit that seeped into her every utterance. She captivated men as diverse as Noël Coward and Ernest Hemingway (who always carefully gave the *impression* that they were lovers), and seduced women effortlessly. An aggressive sexual predator, she even once offered to wash Mae West's hair for her. West, who was hetero to a fault, said later, "I didn't let her. I knew *which* hair she wanted to wash."

A movie career as a heavy (notably the murderous neighbor in *Rear Window*) seemed to be Raymond Burr's lot until the 1950s, when his career blossomed like a flower. As the one and only Perry Mason, he became one of the biggest stars of television's golden age. The man had an unbelievable success rate in the courtroom. Well, I mean, with those burning black eyes boring into one, who *wouldn't* 'fess up? When the program was reborn later with the hopelessly lightweight Monte Markham in the role, it died like the mayfly. And Burr? He simply moved on to another success, *Ironside.* His personal life was discreetly gay, and the story given to the public, of a tragic widower who also lost a son, seems to have been pure flackery.

ecil Beaton was a photographer whose work embraced the exquisite (fashion and portraiture) and the gritty (the effects of World War II on his beloved London). He also brought his refined sensibilities to the screen as costume and scenic designer for a number of fine films. *Gigi* and *My Fair Lady* were two of the most lavish, and when we try to evoke those delightful confections in our heads, it's Beaton's visions we see. In his lively diaries he described his famous love affair with Garbo (which was mostly in his *own* head). One day they sat by the pool, wearily discussing the ravages of age. Beaton complained about his sexual organs shrinking. Garbo looked more doleful than usual and finally said, "Oh ... if only I could say the same."

Hattie McDaniel's career demonstrates that an actor can make a quite respectable career out of playing stereotypes. If those are the only roles available, by God, *take* them, and make them glow. Her simple dignity elevated her gallery of maids and mammies above their writing. McDaniel started out as a singer in a band, and was the first black woman to sing on American radio, on hit programs like Eddie Cantor's. She got her own program, too, starring as *Beulah.* Another first came when she played Mammy in *Gone with the Wind.* It resulted in her being the first African-American to win an Oscar, as Best Supporting Actress. Not bad for 1939, winning over even her radiant costar Olivia de Havilland. McDaniel was allegedly one of Tallulah Bankhead's conquests.

When Ricky Nelson grew into adolescence on TV's *The Adventures of Ozzie and Harriet*, the teenage girls of America took note of his dark eyelashes and sexy curl of the lip (a few of us teenage boys noticed, too), and a new Elvis-in-embryo was born. He quickly became the chief draw on the program, easily upstaging his cute but hardly compelling parents. He never was a great singer. It wasn't necessary. His rock-'n'-roll career was built mostly on his looks, some good songs, but mostly on good hard work. He went both ways, and toyed with drugs, but he just couldn't parlay this potentially great copy into real stardom. Not even his death by drugs in an airplane accident could *quite* catapult him into legend.

John Gielgud may not have seized the laurels as the greatest actor of our age (those belong to Olivier), but he was indisputably the greatest speaker of Shakespeare's verse, as even Lord Larry was pleased to acknowledge. At home on a stage since 1921, he has distinguished himself as a stage director too, a writer on theatre, *and* a sensitive film actor. Once, he was arrested for soliciting sex in a public lavatory. The gutter press, naturally, went into feeding-frenzy mode. After the ordeal he returned to the play he was rehearsing. Dame Edith Evans, to break the ice, announced, in that voice like sugar-coated thunder, "Well, Johnny, I hear you've been a *naughty boy!* Now! ... Let's get back to work." Gielgud's relief must have been immense.

Every elementary school in America has one kid who's willing to eat a cockroach or something equally repugnant. You know, to shock the girls, get attention ... whatever. In certain schools in Baltimore, the kid *had* to be John Waters, the poet of upchuck. A mind like this has to erupt into either psychosis or art, right? I guess we all got lucky. You got a choice between a lone gunman at the top of a school tower or the sight of a mountainous transvestite eating doggy-doo, *most* people would choose the latter. Even if these days he seems to have gone almost respectable on us, with flicks like *Hairspray* and *Serial Mom*, his name still evokes the nightmare delights of Divine in eruption, the heady popcorn scent of the midnight matinee.

Gertrude Lawrence's voice had the romantic throb of a violin, but tended to go *terribly* flat at the end of a vocal line. The public didn't care. They didn't even *notice* her vocal shortcomings, so bewitched were they by her acting genius. Even Noël Coward, the most exacting of critics, wrote: "I had the advantage of playing *Private Lives* with Gertrude Lawrence, so three-quarters of the battle was won before the curtain went up." Moving to America, she made Broadway hers, from the early *Charlot's Revue*, to her final appearance in *The King and I*. Her movie appearances were sporadic, but the last role was a plum: Amanda Wingfield in *The Glass Menagerie*. Basically hetero, Lawrence was cheerfully willing to experiment, indulging in a brief affair with novelist Daphne du Maurier.

You knew it, I knew it, *everybody* knew it, by the way the actor's eyes almost melted out of their sockets whenever James Dean was in the same frame. In *Rebel without a Cause,* Sal Mineo was every sweet, shy kid who ever idolized the captain of the football team. Still, he knew how to make his soft Italianate beauty work for him, and was nominated for supporting actor Oscars twice. But after a bit, the choice roles started falling to others. So he turned back to acting for the stage, where he'd gotten his start, and directing the drama of prison rape, *Fortune and Men's Eyes.* But at thirty-seven, he was stabbed to death in an alley, after rehearsing a play. The murder is still unsolved.

In his youth Tyrone Power was very accurately described as pretty: dark, dewy eyes dripping with inky black lashes; a fine, sensitive mouth. His deep, euphonious voice served him well, too. All these gifts were quite serviceable as a substitute for talent. The son of a commanding stage actor, Power was something of a washout as an actor onscreen, but played a husband with some conviction. His three marriages were covers, of course, like many Tinseltown *ménages.* It was only after his looks started to coarsen that he was able to rise above the pretty-boy image. His sleazy husband in *Witness for the Prosecution* was a beautifully detailed performance. It seemed to be the harbinger of real acting promise, but the next year he was dead of a heart attack.

Some men are simply *not* born for Levi's. Clifton Webb started out on Broadway as a sinuous wisp of a dancer and singer with a light, reedy tenor voice. A series of dramatic roles brought him to Hollywood during the silent era, but he was soon back onstage, and didn't return to the screen for twenty years. His comeback role was triumphant: the acerbic Waldo Lydecker in *Laura*, that perfect *film noir*. And a star was reborn. Clifton was the pampered darling of one of the great clinging mothers, the infamous Mabelle. She was his best girl, his mainstay, his perennial date. When she died — in her nineties — poor Clifton was inconsolable. Remarked Noël Coward astringently, "It's tough to be orphaned at seventy."

Montgomery Clift must have grown fervently sick of being referred to as sensitive. But he practically held the copyright on that quality, even in an unsympathetic role like Morris Townsend in *The Heiress.* A spellbinding beauty in his youth, he enraptured both men and women. Everyone wanted to possess him, to protect and cherish him; men won. Clift never made peace with his homosexuality, seeking to numb his confusion with liquor and drugs. And as a result, even his beauty was taken from him; while making *Raintree County* he drunkenly slammed his car into a tree, disfiguring his face. The abuse problems mounted, and he became sexual prey for anyone sober enough to take him on in the low bars he frequented. A fatal heart attack mercifully finished the job.

What is it about the English? Why have they produced so many virtuoso romantic actors? The darkly introspective Sir Michael Redgrave began onstage but was comfortable in film too, unnerving as the tormented ventriloquist in *Dead of Night*, a convincing hero in *The Lady Vanishes*. Redgrave married the exquisite Rachel Kempson. She had affairs with other men. That was all right; he did too. Together, though, they created a theatrical dynasty: a son Corin, daughters Lynn and Vanessa, and an equally gifted granddaughter, Natasha Richardson. Redgrave was cool and distant to his children, as Lynn relates in her one-woman show *Shakespeare for My Father*. But in one of his last movies, *The Go-Between*, he was able to tap into this frosty detachment, playing a man unable to connect with others.

Hollywood's first major female director was Dorothy Arzner, born on the third day of the new century. Her father owned a small cafe in Hollywood, where Dorothy waited tables, and where she made her first film contacts. She began as a lowly stenographer, then script clerk, then writer and film editor. Her innovative cutting caught the eye of director James Cruze, and by 1927 she herself was directing. A forthright lesbian, she rose by her own merits, not in the hallowed Hollywood manner of assuming position Y. Arzner directed some top female stars — Clara Bow in *The Wild Party*, Katharine Hepburn in *Christopher Strong*, and Joan Crawford in *The Bride Wore Red* — but she stopped cold in 1943, finishing her career producing WAC training films for World War II.

How convincing can drag be when a man has a face like an indignant Labrador retriever? With a luxuriant mustache, yet. Toothy, irreverent Billy De Wolfe's secret lay in not *being* convincing. Few performers could seize the stage from an exotic eccentric like Hermione Gingold, but De Wolfe found it easy. He had only to don a flowery frock or sail into his "lady taking a bath" routine to rise above a whole *stageful* of zanies. This dragmeister *extraordinaire* made terrific movies too, like *Call Me Madam*. But even a gifted clown can play it straight occasionally; he was J.B. Biggley in the London production of *How to Succeed in Business without Really Trying*. The audience may have seen De Wolfe sporting a tailored suit, but underneath? Pure Maidenform!

Everybody's favorite 300-pound transvestite is — need you ask? — *Divine!* The elephantine vixen was christened, simply, Harris Glenn Millstead. But his high school pal, filmmaker John Waters, saw more than a tubby kid. Still, Harris Glenn Millstead as Francine Fishpaw in *Polyester?* Nawww ... *too* prosaic. Besides, did Michelangelo need more than one name? Did Liberace? Did Trigger? Divine, with its divinity and *fudge* connotations, was simply, splendidly right. He was one gutsy actor. I mean, would *you* bend down and scoop poodle poop up in a steaming handful, only to chow down on the loathsome mess? *Pink Flamingos* was a stunning breakthrough in barf-bag filmmaking. Ahhh, but this bag of talent was not content merely to act; he toured as a singer, too, with the band Divine Intervention.

Do all Welshmen have such voices? Emlyn Williams had only one rival in basic vocal equipment, but he wasn't even in film: Dylan Thomas. *Another* Welshman. Williams was a writer too, of several fine plays, including the classic, autobiographical *The Corn is Green.* He also wrote screenplays, a study of murder *(Beyond Belief),* and two volumes of memoirs. In *Emlyn,* he frankly related the story of his love affair with an older, alcoholic actor. His hot, ardent eyes, dramatic intensity, and rich, rolling delivery of lines insured his constant employment as an actor. But because Joseph von Sternberg failed to complete the film *I, Claudius,* we tragically missed seeing Williams as the mad Caligula, that *highly* unbalanced, screaming queen. It must have been a *spectacle.*

In 1948, American audiences just wanted to have fun and forget the war. They wanted a *hunk,* not a great actor: handsome former truck driver Rock Hudson. His first movie was *Fighter Squadron* and it took him thirty-eight takes to get his first line right. His skills as an actor grew quickly but he was mostly famous for his jeans-creaming good looks. Weepies *(Magnificent Obsession),* action films *(Bengal Brigade),* melodramas (the sublimely turgid *Written on the Wind)* — he made forty movies before striking gold in 1959: trying to get into Doris Day's panties in a series of bright sex farces. Unhappily, his late career was darkened when he was dragged out of the closet in the cruelest way, as the first major actor to succumb to AIDS.

Grandpa Walton, *gay?* Yup. Will Geer had a long and distinguished career onstage before turning, more or less permanently, to film in the late forties. He was a great character actor, generally playing cantankerous or sinister types, often in westerns. But in 1951 he was blacklisted for failing to name names, under duress by the Great Inquisition conducted by the House Un-American Activities Committee. Many fine careers were destroyed by that obscene travesty of democracy at work, but Geer bounced back. Eight years later, Otto Preminger defied the blacklist and hired him for *Advice and Consent.* The film rather sensationalized homosexuality, but Geer was back on track. He added television to his résumé, and returned to his roots, the stage, in the Broadway musical *110 in the Shade.*

Seeing Harvey Fierstein onstage in his tour de force *Torch Song Trilogy,* you won't quite believe your eyes. Gay stereotypes have provided no clues as to what to expect. To begin with, he's big — and very imposing. And when he opens his mouth...! My God, that *voice.* It's part croak, part pussycat purr, part sonic boom, rich in pathos and dignity. It was inevitable that Hollywood should attempt to translate this dazzling play to celluloid — and just as inevitable that they should fail. Even with Fierstein recreating the role of Arnold it somehow felt a little thin, rather lost on the wide, sunny screen. Since then, all too typically, film folk haven't known *quite* how to use him, allowing this titan to fritter away his genius as comic relief.

Alla Nazimova was the undisputed queen of a coterie of lesbian actresses in the days of silent film. She was also one of the first stage stars to embrace the infant medium with respectful enthusiasm; in those days, the Lords of the Theatre would rather admit to bayonetting babies than doing *film* work. A great original, Nazimova played more naturalistically onstage, but when she hit her mark before a camera, Byzantium was once again in flower. Her version of *Salome,* with costumes and sets by the visionary Natasha Rambova, was like a fever dream from the sweat-bespangled brow of Aubrey Beardsley. In 1925 she retired from film, but returned, visiting royalty, to play a few character roles in the forties.

Luchino Visconti, born into the Olympian heights of the Italian nobility, need hardly have worked at all. Still, le Conte di Modrone, as he was listed in the *Almanach de Gotha*, tumbled into the artistic ferment of Paris, and *la vie Boheme* did the rest. Working as a costume designer and assistant to the great Jean Renoir, he became drenched in passion for film. Away from Mussolini's oppressive regime, Visconti became a dedicated Communist, almost as if to dissociate himself further from his aristocratic milieu. But he didn't stray so far that he couldn't examine it thoroughly in *The Leopard*. That film may have been his most personal artistic statement, but late in his career, he also explored his homosexuality, in stately fantasias like *The Damned* and *Death in Venice*.

Paul Lynde started out onstage in the musical revue *New Faces of 1952*, writing *and* performing. When he played the Ed Sullivan–infatuated Mr. McAfee in *Bye Bye Birdie*, Hollywood wisely imported him for the film version. He stayed to inject much-needed vinegar into several frothy comedies of the early sixties — and never returned to the stage. When TV beckoned, he abandoned movies, too. Ah, well, the easy money of being a television "personality" isn't exactly to be despised. *Especially* when you can sneakily introduce gay humor into middle America's very living room. In the early days of *Hollywood Squares* only Lynde could get away with a quip like the following. Question: Why do the Hell's Angels wear black leather? Lynde's deliciously malicious answer: Because chiffon *wrinkles* so easily.

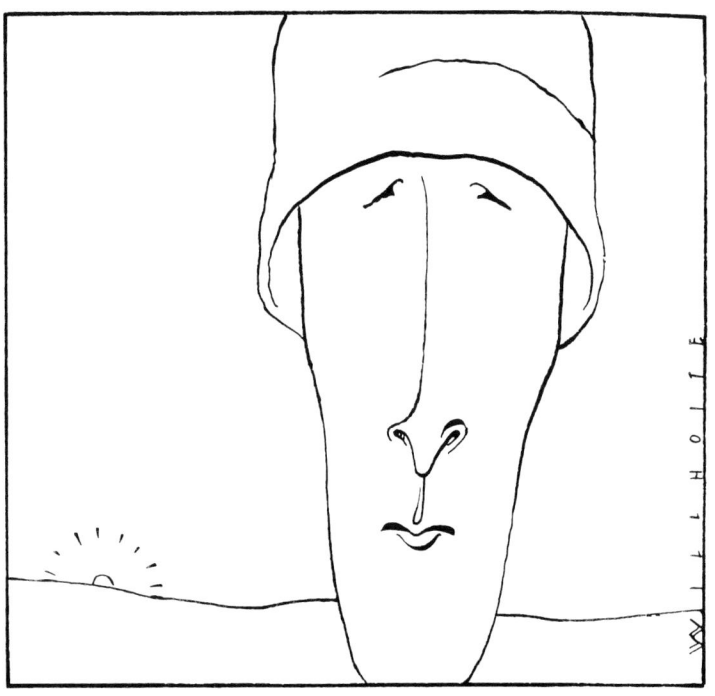

Germany's silent film director F.W. Murnau *(Nosferatu)* began brilliantly — and got even better. *The Last Laugh,* a heartless tragicomedy, was unusual for its time: it completely dispensed with subtitles without sacrificing narrative clarity. Hollywood, disregarding tradition, actually recognized his genius. They imported him. When filmmakers are polled as to the greatest movies of all time, Murnau's first American film *Sunrise* always makes the list. But, alas, it was to be the end of a great career. He had just finished *Tabu,* which would be an astounding success. He never knew it: the week before the premiere, he died in an auto accident. Legend has it that Murnau was going down on his chauffeur at the time. Hey, if you simply *have* to die in a car crash...

John Garfield was a special actor, one who, tough as leather, could *still* break your heart. Like Cagney and Bogart, he was the quintessential city boy, vulnerable, cynical, but with a romantic's heart. He always seemed to play the type who started out on the wrong side of the tracks, and by dint of hard work and the love of a good woman ... stayed there. Garfield died of a heart attack, in the arms (or legs, if you like) of a young woman, *à la* Nelson Rockefeller. Somehow it seemed characteristic. Yeah, his credentials as a straight guy were pretty impeccable, *but* Truman Capote claimed to have nailed him once. (I know, I know, ol' Tru claimed a *lot* of such conquests, but he can't have been lying *every* time...)

O nstage early in the century, Franklin Pangborn was a dramatic actor, even playing such relentlessly butch roles as the villainous Messala in *Ben-Hur*. Then he reached the screen. One of his first movies was *Getting Gertie's Garter*, and from then on, he was typed in comedy. So, what the hell — you play what you can. The parts he got were hotel clerks and officious salesmen, or thankless organizers who always seemed to end up humiliated or more flustered. His dithery, blissfully prissy presence brightened many a comedy throughout the thirties and forties. Like Eric Blore, Edward Everett Horton, and a host of similar players, he was never a star. Usually not even identifiable by name, he was always familiar, always welcome, and *always* employed.

Janet Gaynor, a sweet, plucky little sparrow in silent films, was paired with Charles Farrell in a series of romantic movies in the early days of sound. They must have been amused to find themselves sex symbols, especially together. Both were gay (though she married repeatedly — once to the dress designer Adrian). Gaynor started as a bit player, but within a year she was the biggest star on the Fox lot. She was the first actress to win an Oscar, not for one film, as became customary, but for her collective work on *Sunrise, Seventh Heaven,* and *Street Angel.* In 1938 she retired but returned to film one more time, unable to resist the temptation to play Pat Boone's mother (egad!) in *Bernadine.*

English director John Schlesinger views the American scene with an unusually unclouded eye. His movie *Midnight Cowboy,* twenty-five years after its premiere, is still fresh, still jarring, and not *remotely* dated. Events have made Ratso and Joe's homelessness more resonant than originally, but the graphic gay sex can still startle, even after the past quarter century's sexual candor onscreen. Still, in this movie and *Sunday, Bloody Sunday,* the emotional content is more important than the sexual. Schlesinger, in spite of a 27-year relationship with producer-photographer Michael Childers, recently came out, and is now working on an AIDS project. As he's always more than ready to twist the tails of the politically correct, I confidently predict that he'll continue to surprise some and — bless him — enrage others.

A cuddly bear with a yummy plum pudding of a voice, Simon Callow is recognizable as one of the Merchant-Ivory repertory players, and works steadily in other films, too. (In Mike Newell's *Four Weddings and a Funeral*, a particularly florid performance, his alliance with John Hannah is portrayed as simply another couple relationship; imagine the knowing smirk with which most American directors would have handled the same situation.) And he has a growing reputation in Britain as a stage director and classically trained actor. It's too little known that Callow is a superb writer. *Being an Actor*, partly professional memoir, gives invaluable insights into the craft of acting. But Callow's finest accomplishment — on the page, that is — may be his superlative biography of Charles Laughton, another lavishly gifted gay actor.

The Scottish actor Ian Charleson started out as all true sons of Britain do, in Shakespeare. As a mere tot of twenty-six, he tackled that actor's Everest, the back-breaking role of Hamlet, but with his slender blond beauty he was more felicitously cast as Ariel in *The Tempest.* He tried musicals too, as a dreamy, lightweight Sky Masterson in *Guys and Dolls.* His looks were natural for film, and he made a good first impression in *Gandhi* and *Greystoke, the Legend of Tarzan.* The role he'll be remembered for, though, is the prickly, would-be saint Eric Liddell in *Chariots of Fire.* But Charleson was too beautiful to last. He had only begun to make his mark when he succumbed to AIDS, another of our many great losses.

Howard Hughes was once a true Prince of Hollywood. As a young man-about-Tinseltown, he produced and directed fourteen movies and launched the careers of several actresses. He was seen escorting stars like Harlow, Hepburn, Gardner, and Rogers, but never *quite* made it official. (One reason was his bisexuality; rumor had it that Hughes was one of Errol Flynn's conquests.) The bashful billionaire's influence on the film industry wasn't always benign: when he bought the once-great studio RKO in 1948, he caused the company to collapse through capricious whim and mismanagement. In later years, he became known for his epic eccentricities, obscene wealth, five-inch fingernails, and hysterical mysophobia. If T.S. Eliot could find fear in a handful of dust, Hughes found something akin to terror.

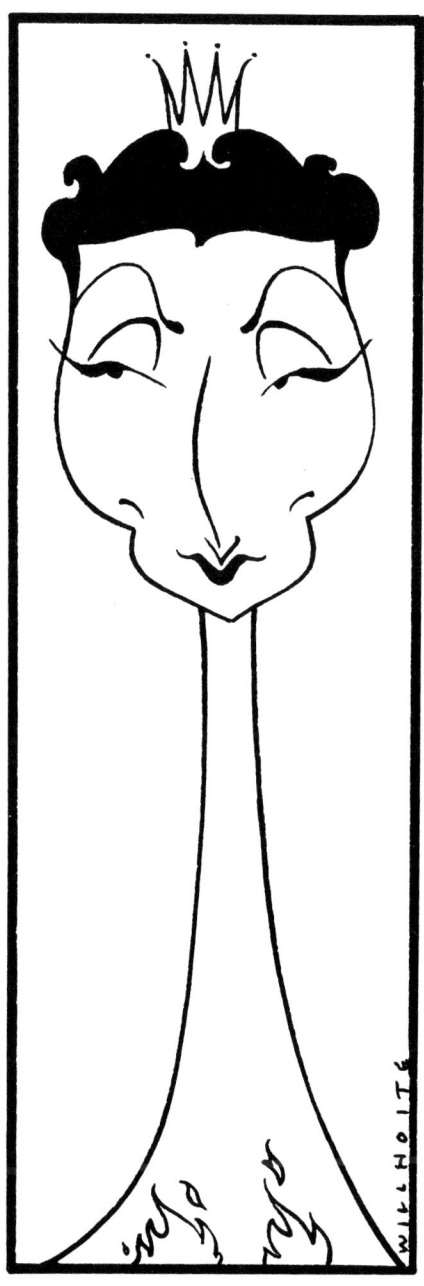

Brittle wits and thin-lipped neurotics, raddled hags and imperious courtesans: Agnes Moorehead could probably have been convincing playing a fire hydrant. She was nominated for an Oscar in only her second film, *The Magnificent Ambersons,* as Tim Holt's bitter spinster aunt (her first had been the small but telling role of young Citizen Kane's stoic mother). Four other nominations followed. She played a slatternly housekeeper in *Hush, Hush ... Sweet Charlotte,* an elegant witch on television, and a witty, discarded mistress in Bernard Shaw's *Don Juan in Hell.* Clearly a class act in any role. She even hit the airwaves, in the gripping radio play *Sorry, Wrong Number.* Two hundred world cities saw this simply wonderful actress touring in her one-woman show, *The Fabulous Redhead.* And who could disagree?

F<i>rankenstein</i> — the movie, not the monster — was brought to life by James Whale, an Englishman who found the American studio system more congenial. Contradictory to his name, Whale was trim and dapper, a magician who infused even his horror films with killer wit. The choicest example: *The Bride of Frankenstein*, one of the most delightful (there's no other word) of creature features. It scintillates throughout — even the framing device, in which Elsa Lanchester, who plays perky Mary Shelley, also takes the role of Karloff's sweet intended, that satanic mechanical bird. Whale was very open about his sexual persuasion, and ended up, like William Holden in *Sunset Boulevard*, floating face-downward in his swimming pool. He was written off as a suicide, but foul play was possibly involved.

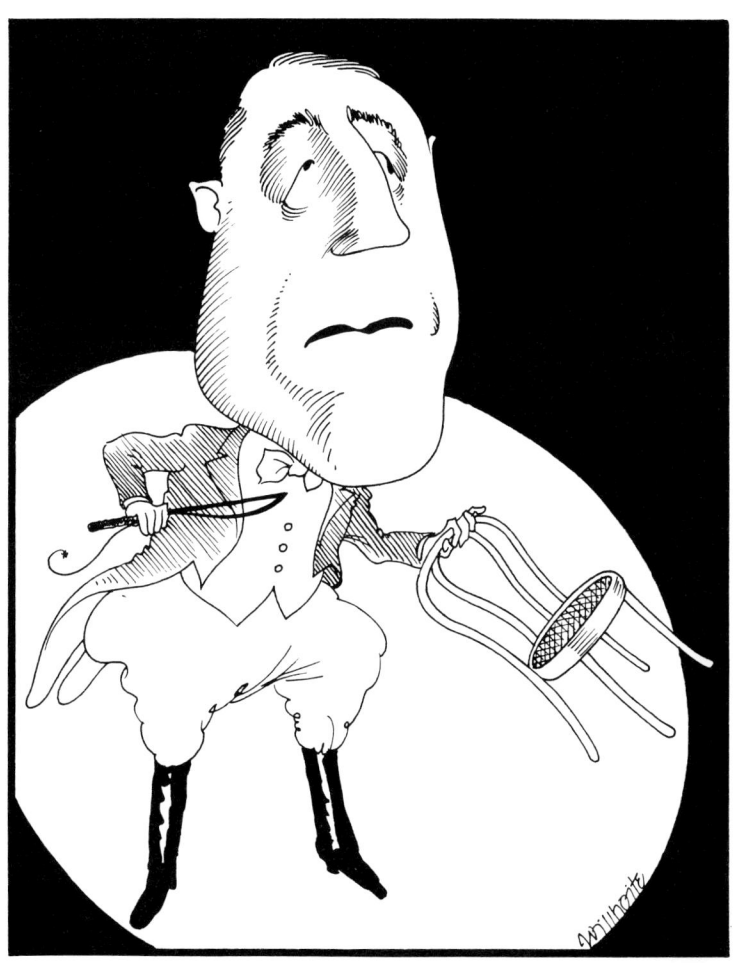

Patrick McGilligan, writing of George Cukor, baldly claims he was the only major director who was gay. Not so. There were others, like Edmund Goulding, whom some unfairly dismiss as a journeyman. Even if he had no distinct personal style, he could easily adopt the house style of the various studios who employed him. Let's give him this, too: He *definitely* won his spurs directing the temperamental Bette Davis in some of the glossier items in her résumé. *And* Garbo. *And* Fontaine. And other stellar tigresses. Oh, they were *not* pussycats in those days! A gentle, cultivated man, Goulding started as a screenwriter, and continued writing even as he directed. An able composer, he could even turn out a theme song for one of his last assignments, *Teenage Rebel*.

Playing a Diana Vreeland–like fashion editor in *Funny Face*, Kay Thompson came close to stealing the show from old pro Fred Astaire and the thrillingly beautiful young Audrey Hepburn. Her elegant croaking of "Think Pink" opened the movie, as a flotilla of models floated about her. Kay was primarily a nightclub performer, smoke and martinis seeping into every corner of her throaty voice, but every now and then she dabbled in movies, like *Tell Me That You Love Me, Junie Moon*. This last starred Liza Minnelli, the daughter of her friend Judy Garland (Kay being one of the women Garland was allegedly linked with romantically). But her greatest fame came as the author of *Eloise*, that one-of-a-kind children's classic.

Wayland Flowers would have been the first to claim he was no ventriloquist, just a clever straight man (okay then, *gay* man) to the rudest top banana in the world. Now that he's no longer with us, the ugly truth can be told: the gentleman moved his lips. Well, I don't suppose it mattered much. After all, cute as he was, nobody *really* looked at him. They couldn't keep their eyes off that impudent hussy on his lap: Madame. A randy old broad, a geriatric floozy, the pleasure principle in three-inch eyelashes, Madame was perfectly willing, honey, to say *exactly* what she thought. And, boy, did gay audiences lap it up. Even straights who wandered in by mistake found themselves laughing helplessly.

Dolores Del Rio was one of the most gorgeous women ever to be projected upon the screen, the equal of Garbo or Vivien Leigh. This orchidaceous beauty was imported from Mexico in the silent era, but when sound came she found herself frequently typecast because of her accent. She was still popular well into the forties but only in a musical soufflé like *Flying Down to Rio* was she able to rise above the ethnic trap. When this elegant lesbian's marriage of convenience to MGM's famous set designer Cedric Gibbons ended in the early forties, she repaired to Mexico, and her career soared, on screen and stage. She couldn't really stay away from Hollywood completely, even returning to play Elvis Presley's mother (!) in his best movie, *Flaming Star*.

More than simply Del Rio's cover, Cedric Gibbons was probably the finest and most influential designer in film history. (He's the only production designer whose name I've heard applauded in the credits: *admittedly,* in a theatre full of screaming movie queens.) Starting out with Edison in 1915, he moved to MGM in 1924 and was quickly recognized as the chief architect of the studio's visual style. He designed for dozens of great pictures. Consult any film encyclopedia and marvel; one classic film right after another: *Ben-Hur* (silent); *Private Lives; Grand Hotel; Mutiny on the Bounty; Camille; Gaslight; Ninotchka; Pride and Prejudice; Little Women; On the Town; An American in Paris; The Bad and the Beautiful.* Gibbons was the proud winner of a dozen Oscars — the statue he himself designed.

Tall, horsy, and plain, Dan Dailey had to make it on talent alone. Vaudeville, burlesque, he slogged through the small-time before hitting Broadway. A small part in Rodgers and Hart's *Babes in Arms* paid off: two years later he was playing opposite Ethel Merman. *Stars in Your Eyes* was one of her rare flops, but it paid off for Dailey. As his film career started, wartime came and took a five-year bite out of it. But he bounced back in a number of Fox musicals. They weren't blockbusters, just good clean fun, often costarring the delicious Betty Grable. In one, *When My Baby Smiles at Me,* he even got an Oscar nomination, but this fine gay song-and-dance man still never got the material he deserved.

Camp was born on the day Beatrice Lillie first sang the quaint Edwardian song "There Are Fairies at the Bottom of Our Garden" before a grateful audience. This Canadian comedienne, her hair in a thoroughly butch bob, remained resolutely feminine, whether cavorting about like a demented goose or daintily munching an ear of buttered corn while wearing elbow-length gloves. She garnered her greatest raves onstage but also made a handful of movies, most of them unworthy of her deliciously oddball talent. However, in a subsidiary role like the sinister Mrs. Meers in *Thoroughly Modern Millie,* she could still rip a picture out from under such competition as Julie Andrews — and even the flamboyant Carol Channing. A discreet lesbian, she nonetheless married into the British nobility, becoming Lady Peel.

Mexican-born Ramon Novarro was Valentino's greatest rival as "Latin lover" on the silent screen. Women found his pouting, troubled quality irresistible. And they wanted to see him *undressed*. So his directors shrewdly shot him as nearly nude as conventions of the day would allow. (Bathing and dressing scenes were *permissibly* lubricious.) But female fans could only dream: Novarro was gay, with a pronounced appetite for rough trade. By his late career, he was reduced to scattered bit parts, but the manner of his death assured him a kind of posthumous fame. At age sixty-nine, he was beaten to death in his own home by two young hustlers. Yet art can provide a coda: this sad ending was transmuted into "Tango," a haunting song by Lieber and Stoller.

Albert Dekker was a fine actor whose most characteristic roles, like Dr. Cyclops, were a little on the spooky side. Still, his weirdest role was that of California assemblyman in the 57th District for two years. (Alas, it would be another actor, the even *more* nightmarish Ronald Reagan, who had the more permanent political career.) Dekker stayed in film, making a modest name for himself. But, unfortunately, his devils caught up with him. How terrible to be always remembered for the manner of one's suicide. His body was found bound, handcuffed, and hanging from his shower curtain rod. His final costume was a lovely ensemble of lacy lingerie. The suicide note, if you can call it that, was written on himself, in lipstick. Wow. Talk about "going out in style..."

MICHAEL WILLHOITE

She is obsidian and alabaster, a study in contrasts. Cynical, amused eyes glitter above a tight red mouth, contemptuous of the lusts of those men who would use her — were they intelligent enough. She is Louise Brooks, a celluloid sphinx. She makes a few movies, usually as a heartless, heedless flapper, flaming youth. Then she deserts Hollywood forever, flees to Germany to make two films for G.W. Pabst, *Diary of a Lost Girl* and *Pandora's Box.* The reputation crystallizes into legend. Sound arrives, she makes a few more films, and leaves the party. Her only further contact with film is at the end of her life. The elegant, elderly wraith gives a few tart, articulate interviews and writes trenchantly on film. And no man knows her.

In the great golden days of the silent screen, a wedding could be as grandiose a production as Griffith's *Intolerance*. One of the gaudiest of these spectacles was that of Rod La Rocque and Vilma Banky, a pageant masterminded by Samuel Goldwyn, the man who made La Rocque famous. Yes, Rod La Rocque. (Oooh ... so *phallic*. And his real name.) It was even a happy marriage of sorts. God knows it was a long one, with him in the west wing and her in the east. (Or the other way around. But you get the idea.) This yummy matinee idol made an easy transition to sound, and made a modest fortune. But before age blasted his beauty, he gave up acting — to become even richer in real estate.

No movie director interprets Verdi's operas and Shakespeare's Italian romances as sensitively as Franco Zeffirelli; it's genetic. He started as an actor (those looks!), and under Luchino Visconti's magisterial influence, staged operas and designed sets and costumes. By the late sixties, this magician was ready to conquer film. In *The Taming of the Shrew* and *Romeo and Juliet,* the golden light of Italy shimmers off the screen. His filming of Otello and *La Traviata,* dripping with visual and aural opulence, could make a confirmed operaphobe moisten his knickers. Still, even a master can come a cropper from time to time. Zeffirelli's filming of *Endless Love* is practically a classic of how *not* to make a picture. But what the hell, *you* try to bring a Brooke Shields performance to life.

Hoffman. De Niro. Duvall. Malkovich. What do these actors have in common? Sure, they're the best we have, all loners, ferocious individualists. But the real common denominator is what they owe to Marlon Brando. He set the standard then as he sets it now. In the fifties, when he burst onto the screen like a petulant young animal, the face of acting was changed forever. (Just remember the generation of impressionists he launched, scratching their chests through torn t-shirts, mumbling, and yawping "STELL-*AAAH!!!*") The great tragedy of his career is that one so prodigiously gifted should have expressed, repeatedly, a sneering contempt for the art of acting. His record with women is well documented, but his frank disclosure that he also goes the other way was something of a bombshell.

Judy Holliday was universally acknowledged as a comic genius. With her champagne blonde hair, deep dimples, *and* razor-sharp timing, she was deliriously goofy — with a sensible center. Her image of a Central Casting dumb blonde hid a formidable intelligence; it also concealed wretched loneliness. Holliday never could quite make up her mind what she wanted. Women, sure, but she also made herself miserable by falling in love with the wrong men. The saxophonist Gerry Mulligan made her fleetingly happy, but she was doomed anyway. An attack by McCarthy's malign forces severely crippled her career, but cancer effectively polished off the rest. In her movies, she spread joy like pollen in springtime. But in the end, she was given precious little herself.

If a martini could have come to life — human life, that is — it might have become Jack Buchanan. This type of suave song-and-dance man, the embodiment of grace and elegance, can no longer be found. It flourished *only* between the wars. He didn't so much sing a song as coo it gently; his dancing was butterfly-light. Buchanan is often characterized as Britain's Fred Astaire, but the description is oddly inadequate. These Olympians could probably never have developed such parallel careers in the same country, without becoming bitter enemies. But the two legends were so self-assured, so perfectly *themselves,* that when they were paired in a delicious film musical, *The Band Wagon,* they enhanced one another's performances. Well, I mean, when gods meet, ego is unnecessary.

It must be nice — for *somebody* — that *The Partridge Family* is back on television. (Shirley Jones groupies?) After all, even militant wholesomeness can be a welcome respite from some of today's confrontational entertainment. But can't we please be spared the smirking face of the rather desiccated David Cassidy flacking for it on-camera? Self-love *does* rather inform his delivery, as it crept into every note of every song he attempted. A genuine if modest talent has unfortunately been somewhat obscured by an immodest personality. He has admitted in an interview to bisexuality. Still, one wonders if that was perhaps a publicity ploy. The TV public's attention span *does* grow more stunted every year, and a little sexual tweak can jolt even a couch potato.

In her early Paramount musicals with Maurice Chevalier *(Love Me Tonight, The Love Parade)*, Jeanette MacDonald was a witty, sexy wench. Chevalier brought out her playful side. MGM, on the other hand, paired her off with a *real* stiff, stolid, humorless, *wholesome* Nelson Eddy. The pair, billed as "America's Singing Sweethearts," starred in a series of gooey operettas, the apotheosis of romantic longing. They *oozed* prestige and made tons of money for an ecstatic Louis B. Mayer (who *demanded* the gay actor get hitched). But wartime, alas, made the films hopelessly antique. *(Another* crime to lay at Hitler's door!) By the time the public had rediscovered these orgies of sweetness and light, Eddy was dead. But since they were now regarded as high camp, it was probably just as well.

Former taxi dancer Rodolfo Alfonzo Raffaele Pierre Philibert Guglielmi (try to fit that onto a marquee) neatly reshaped his name to become screen idol Rudolph Valentino. The man never should have married, *if* you know what I mean. But the fool did it *twice*, both times to lesbians, for God's sake. When he put his career into the hands of his second, she all but wrecked it, deftly snipping away what was left of his balls by feminizing his image. In 1926 a vicious *Chicago Tribune* editorial lambasted him as a "pink powder puff," and "that painted pansy," but before it could hurt his career, he was dead of a perforated ulcer. It set off a national spasm of grief unparalleled until the demise of St. Elvis. Good career move.

The sloe-eyed vamp above is the exotic enchantress Natasha Rambova (née Winifred Shaughnessy of Salt Lake City, Utah). Ludicrously self-absorbed by her flame of creativity, she *did* have a highly original visual sense which she turned to fine account in her set and costume designs — notably for Alla Nazimova's production of *Salome*. She acted in exactly one film, *When Love Grows Cold*, and was so incensed by being billed as *Mrs*. Rudolph Valentino that she quit the screen for good. She turned to the stage, and *barely* escaped being booed off it by the critics. Playwriting, spiritualism, Egyptology ... talk about your energetic dabblers! This last *did* provide her with a fine collection of Egyptian and Far Eastern art — which she willed to museums in Utah and Philadelphia.

In the Broadway musical *Lady in the Dark,* Danny Kaye brought the audience leaping out of their seats with "Tchaikovsky," a song in which he spewed forth the names of fifty-four Russian composers in under a minute. With his elegant wife Sylvia Fine, who wrote much of his best material, he took Hollywood like Pancho Villa took Chihuahua. In movies like *Knock on Wood* and *The Court Jester,* Kaye was a rather specialized taste, inspiring either adoration or queasiness. But when this verbal Roman candle played London, the British simply *worshipped* him. His most devoted fan turned out to be the greatest actor alive, Laurence Olivier. Their affair was known to everyone in London, even their wives, but only after both men were dead did it become common knowledge in America.

Rugged, handsome George Nader had stardom in his grasp. Then his career got derailed by the tabloids. In the 1950s they were not so bold as they are today, but in that fear-saturated decade they had *power*. They had gotten the goods on gay star Rock Hudson, who was in great danger of being exposed. So his studio made a murky bargain: if the press would only leave Rock alone, they would throw someone else to the lions. Hey, Rock was obviously going places fast, George Nader was on a slower track ... why not? So the gutter press got their copy, Rock got his career (and a showcase wife he didn't really want), and Nader got low-budget European flicks. And that's showbiz, folks.

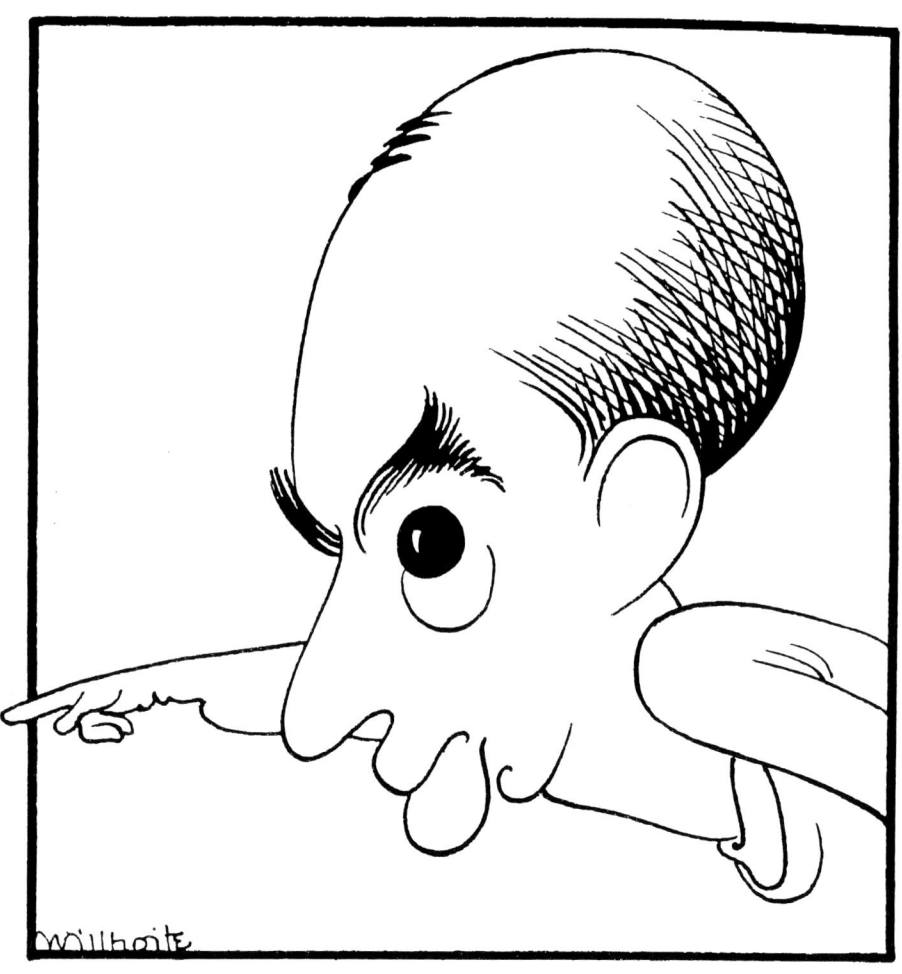

A former Broadway set designer, Vincente Minnelli was drawn inevitably to the film musical. This visual wizard quickly became its greatest master. Fate arrived — in the form of Judy Garland. Artistically, it was a *great* marriage. He coaxed her into a handful of luminescent performances (like the lovely *Meet Me in St. Louis)* but soon her aberrant behavior wrecked their marriage *and* working relationship (his taste for men didn't help, either). Great musicals weren't his only output. In *The Bad and the Beautiful*, a tragically underrated classic, and probably the best film ever made about actual moviemaking, he actually pulled a superior performance out of Lana Turner. His career ended with a dull thud, the execrable *A Matter of Time*, but, dammit, he *still* belongs on Olympus.

Nobody can satisfactorily explain star power. Once on television Judy Garland stood before the camera, her face filling the screen. She sang Charlie Chaplin's song "Smile." Simple. Three minutes, tops. And with face and voice she managed to express more naked emotion, more human longing, more sheer artistry than can be found in *Tosca, Carmen,* and maybe a season of soap opera as well. The sweet little girl who tremulously warbled "Over the Rainbow" became a monster through a succession of disastrous marriages and love affairs (some with women), drugs, and alcohol. A gifted film actress, and probably the greatest saloon singer of them all, she wasn't above alienating her public by tantrums of ego, self-indulgence, and an almost criminal unreliability. But we forgave her everything. She was *ours*.

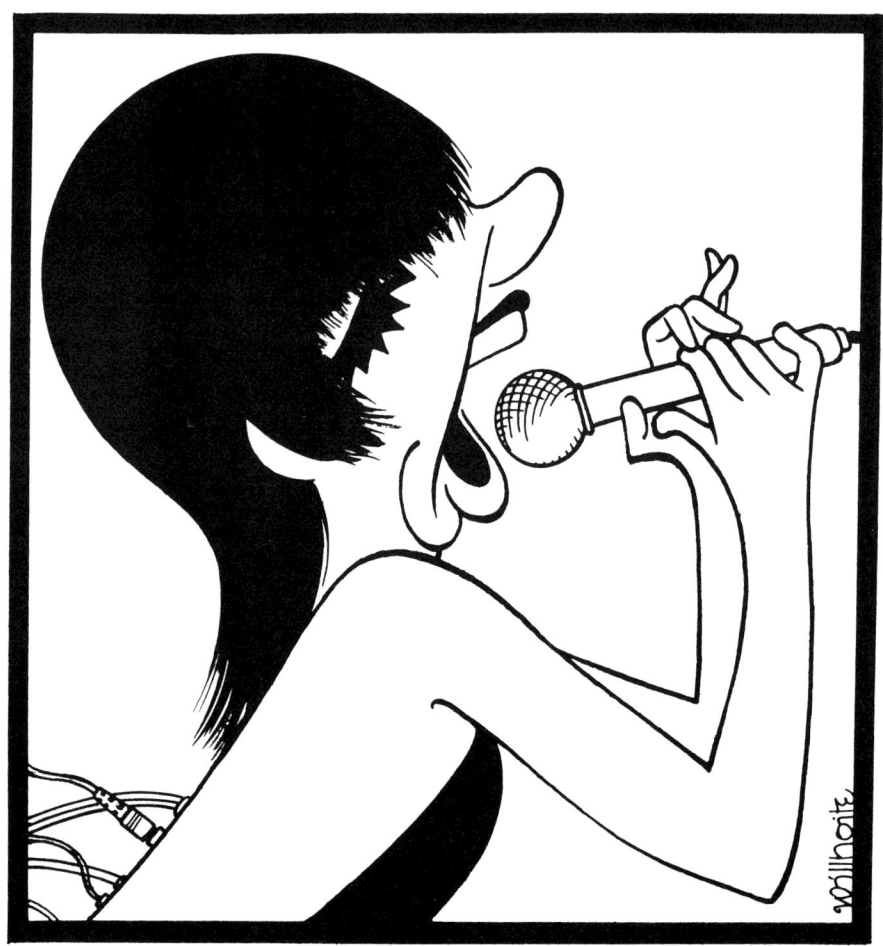

Liza. She's the waif who'll gladly expire onstage, if *only* you'll love her. A history of substance abuse. Worship by millions of gay men. Sound familiar? Liza Minnelli's talent was genetically foreordained. But Mom was, shall we say, a hard act to follow, so Liza wisely got out of town. In New York her first break was a breezy off-Broadway revival of the musical *Best Foot Forward.* Then came *Flora, The Red Menace,* for which she neatly hooked a Tony. Clubs and recordings followed, and a dazzling TV special, *Liza with a Z.* In 1967 she burst into movies. But despite *Cabaret* and *New York, New York,* the scarcity of good musicals has sent Liza back on the personal appearance circuit repeatedly. But it's there that she thrives anyway.

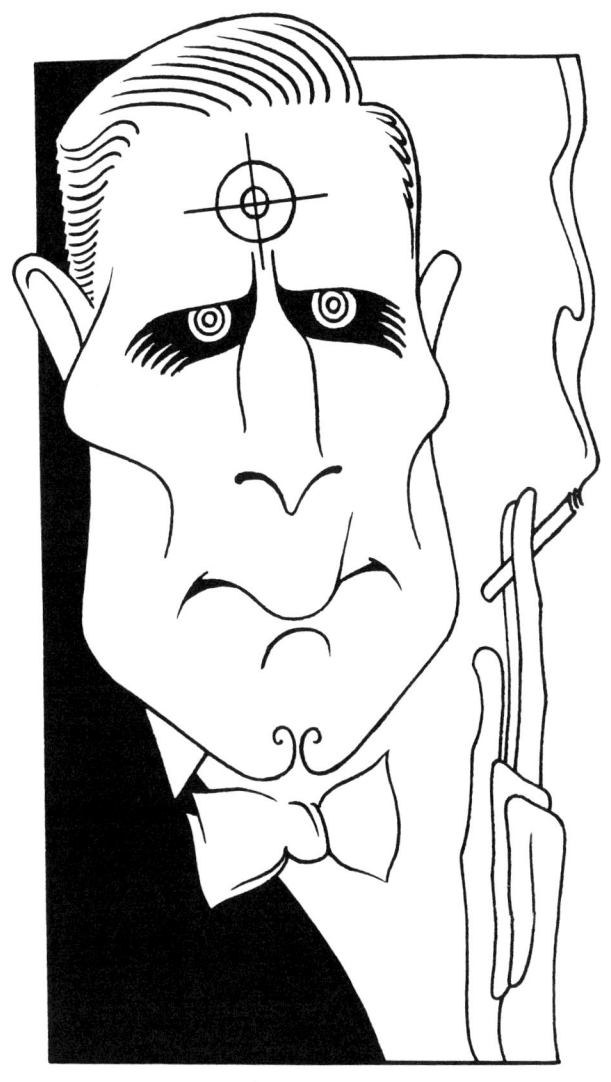

T he director William Desmond Taylor was one of the more rococo characters of the silent era, and the centerpiece of one of its juiciest scandals. Ambisexual, a debaucher of men and women, probably children, and *very* possibly small dogs, he was shot to death in his bungalow one February night in 1922. The case has never been officially solved, but Sidney Kirkpatrick's *A Cast of Killers* makes a wonderfully entertaining stab at it. Not only was his career ended *(very* effectively, you'll agree), but so were those of actresses Mabel Normand and Mary Miles Minter. This last actress was noted for her dewily innocent portrayals. The letters from her to Taylor read aloud at the inquest made a salad of *that* image, you can be sure.

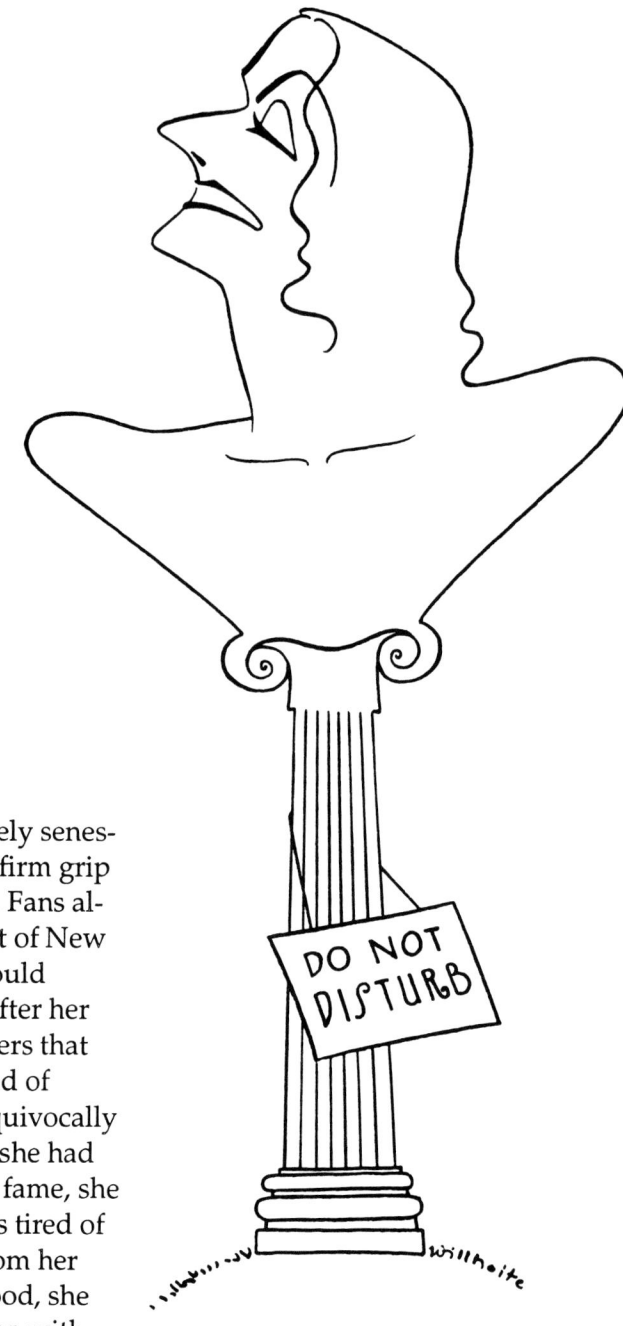

From dimpled youth to lonely senescence, Greta Garbo held a firm grip on the public imagination. Fans always hoped that the Ghost of New York's Upper East Side would return to film, fifty years after her retirement. But despite offers that might have turned the head of Queen Elizabeth, she unequivocally said no. When asked why she had retired at the height of her fame, she only said laconically, "I vas tired of making faces." Brought from her native Sweden to Hollywood, she became an instant superstar, with distinctly mythological overtones. Garbo had an appeal that defies classification or explanation. She has frequently been cited by ordinarily straight women as the one woman they would go to bed with; only a goddess has that kind of power.

Nobody was treated more shabbily by Hollywood than Mauritz Stiller. Considering the gift he bestowed upon the town, this was the stuff of tragedy. A sensitive, innovative director of the Swedish silent screen, Stiller was the first to develop the talent of the very young Greta Garbo. In 1925 he was lured to Hollywood, with Garbo in tow, by Louis B. Mayer. No dummy, Mayer perceived a major star in the making. But he hadn't gotten ahead by tact and sensitivity; he demoted Stiller to assistant director on her first picture. Worse was to come. The gentle gay director was assigned, at Garbo's insistence, to direct *The Temptress,* but was quickly and unceremoniously replaced. He slunk over to Paramount for three films. Dismissed again, Stiller returned to Sweden, dying the following year.

What!? The King ... a *queen*? Well, not exactly. When Clark Gable was a struggling young actor, he went through a period when he was willing to make a few bucks as a male hustler. Now, we can't be *certain* that he went down on producers to oil the wheels of his career, but ... hey, what do hustlers do? (Okay, maybe *some* hustlers only served as bridge partners...) His youthful exploits in our neighborhood perhaps contributed to his later well-known homophobia. Like when he managed to get one director or another fired from pictures he was working on. Nonetheless, Gable was one of a handful of actors of whom homosexuality was never suspected by the public, which in the early days assumed *all* actors were gay.

A fellow student of Cole Porter from their days at Yale, Monty Woolley was also a playmate. If you think we're liberated now, take a dip into the Cole Porter biography by Charles Schwartz. These guys *really* knew how to cruise, taking a jalopy out on balmy evenings for what they demurely described as "fucking parties." Woolley returned to Yale to teach dramatics (one of his students was Thornton Wilder) but quit cold in 1936 to go onstage himself. His role of roles was, of course, the mischievous misanthrope Sheridan Whitesides in *The Man Who Came to Dinner,* which he later brought to the screen. He almost didn't make it, but John Barrymore couldn't learn the lines, so the studio fell back on Woolley's comic genius. *Praises be.*

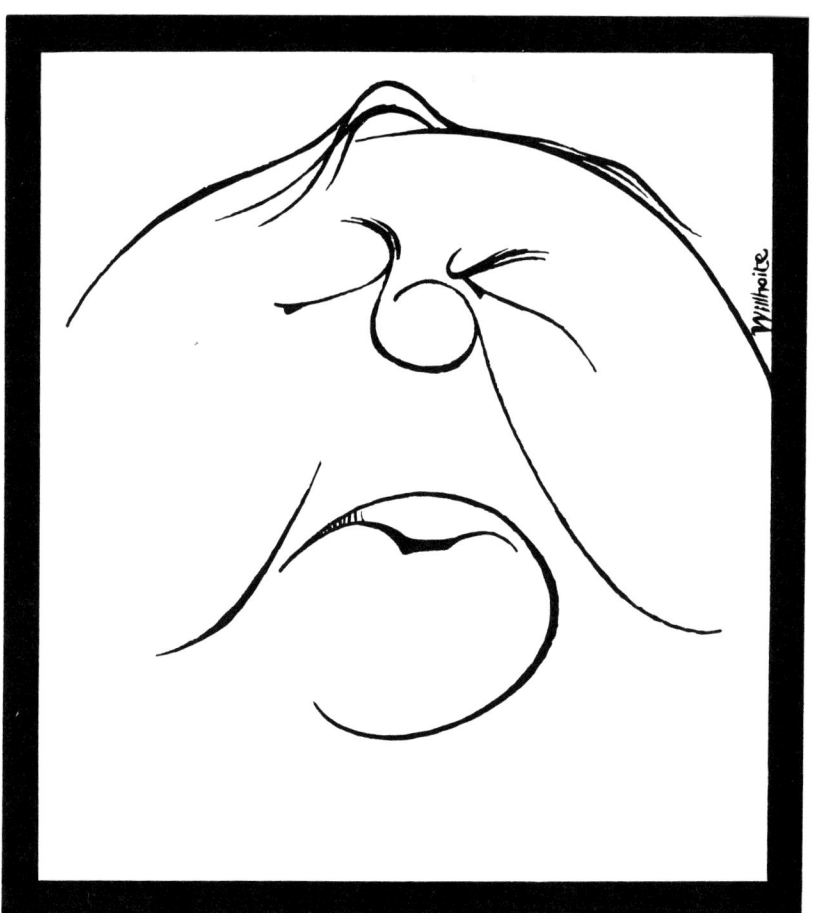

Charles Laughton, a tortured, unhappy genius, hated his body and face. But they were his fortune, a canvas on which he painted a brilliant panoply of roles: a shy butler in *Ruggles of Red Gap;* the chilly Inspector Javert in *Les Miserables;* a hilariously crotchety barrister in *Witness for the Prosecution;* the overbearing fathers of *Hobson's Choice* and *The Barretts of Wimpole Street;* Captain Bligh; Rembrandt; Henry VIII; tycoons; pirates; and most touching of all, the pathetic monster Quasimodo. An actor of great delicacy, he could turn, through boredom or laziness, into a savory, succulent ham. Laughton only went behind the camera once, directing *The Night of the Hunter,* a movie not *remotely* like any other. This visionary masterpiece might have been his finest achievement, but, alas, he never directed another.

Edward Everett Horton was a supreme light comedy actor, but in almost fifty years of film roles, he never got the girl. Hell, he didn't *want* her. He is most fondly remembered as Fred Astaire's sidekick in several of those light-as-meringue musicals of the thirties, but lent his jittery presence to scores of comedies. His character always seemed to be a fussy old maid in britches, *certain* that disaster loomed. He breezed through more than 150 movies, and was popular onstage too, touring for years in the creaky farce *Springtime for Henry*. Later he turned to television, narrating the *Rocky and Bullwinkle* "Fractured Fairy Tales." But his most bizarre casting was as an Indian chief, Roaring Chicken, in the silly sitcom *F Troop*.

Cary Grant. The name conjures up a style, an impeccable skill in comedy or drama, the avatar of grace, *savoir vivre*, and continental charm. Yes, *and* discretion. Grant was gay, no doubt about it, but it was a constant struggle to deny it. Wives *were* collected — though divorces always followed. But his private life is hardly worth commenting upon; what counts is a *most* distinguished career. Grant was equally adept at adventure *(Gunga Din)*, screwball farce *(Bringing Up Baby)*, romantic thrillers *(North by Northwest)*, and glossy cocktail comedy *(The Philadelphia Story)*. But he wasn't above mugging shamelessly through *Arsenic and Old Lace* and *I Was a Male War Bride*, either. This superstar, this matinee idol was not always recognized as one of Hollywood's best actors. But that's *exactly* what he was.

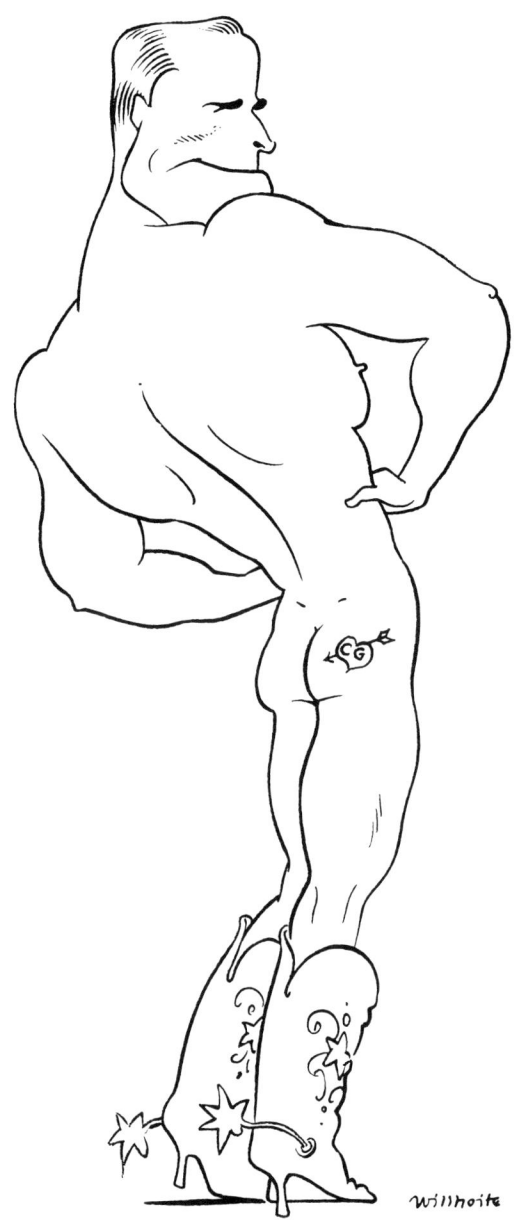

The phrase "ride 'em, cowboy" is given a fresh and utterly irresistible twist when one contemplates the fact that rugged western star Randolph Scott and Cary Grant were once roomies. Rather intimate ones, at that, by the evidence of a magazine spread of the time, the blissfully innocent thirties. In this mind-boggling layout, the two butch stars work together, play together, and gaze raptly at one another across the breakfast table. One almost expects to turn the page and find the duo playing a game of hide-the-sponge or ... well, let's draw a discreet veil over Batman and Robin at this point. Gawd! Try to imagine any two of today's stars in a similar photo feature. Sylvester Stallone? Bruce Willis? Arnold Schwarzenegger? ... No, on second thought, let's *not*.

The late Colin Higgins wanted to be an actor (he *was* handsome), but got sidetracked — by success. His first screenplay was *Harold and Maude,* that black comedy *par excellence.* It became a cult hit, even playing one theatre in Paris for over two years. His next was *Silver Streak,* a throwback to the thirties, and a field day for the extravagant talents of Gene Wilder and Richard Pryor. By his next film, *Foul Play,* Higgins finally had the muscle to direct as well. This playful homage to Hitchcock (one of Chevy Chase's rare *good* movies) led to more directing assignments. Higgins should have stuck to screenwriting. He faltered *badly* halfway through *9 to 5.* And in *The Best Little Whorehouse in Texas,* he unwisely injected seriousness into inspired fluff.

Vaudeville's Sweet Mama Stringbean was a lithe young hedonist, a shimmy on her hips and a song on her lips. As Ethel Waters, she became the first black female headliner on the American stage. When Waters sang the scorching "Heat Wave," not even a stone Aztec god could have remained still. She could sing it blue, too. Her rough-edged wailing of "Stormy Weather" was a howl of pain years before Lena Horne transmuted it into the silken anthem we know. With the movie *Cabin in the Sky* she started edging toward sanctity. Finding Jesus *really* gave the *coup de grace* to her friskiness. By the time she made movies like *Pinky* and *A Member of the Wedding,* she had evolved into a saintly earth mother, a capacious island of calm.

Jack Cassidy *was* handsome, in a disquietingly sleek, frozen-custard way. If one could ignore the too-smooth blandness and that gleaming keyboard of white teeth, one could actually enjoy him. He was a superb singer and sly comic actor, quite willing to poke fun at his own rather alarming prettiness. But Cassidy was *not* a nice man, according to Gerald Clarke's deliciously dishy biography of Truman Capote. Apparently, the actor had a most unlovely relationship with Cole Porter. Cassidy would pull out a favorite appendage, and entice the virtually paraplegic Porter to crawl across the floor for his reward. Ugly, ugly, ugly ... But his end was uglier still. Poor Jack Cassidy, roasting on an open fire, due to his unfortunate habit of smoking in bed.

Leonard Frey originated the role of the Tailor Motel Kamzoil in *Fiddler on the Roof*, onstage and in the movie, a delightful picture of a young man in love. But he was *more* memorable as Harold, the self-described "ugly, pock-marked Jew fairy" in the stage and film versions of Mart Crowley's infamous *The Boys in the Band*. Sure, the movie is embarrassingly dated in its gay self-hate, but something in Frey's playing of Harold, certainly the least attractive of the characters, invites an odd sympathy. When he stood at the door and coldly lacerated himself, oozing self-loathing, he was a gay Everyman, railing against his fate, and taking sour, defiant pride in himself at the same time. Unforgettable.

Howard Ashman, with straight composer Alan Menken, created a modest little show, *Little Shop of Horrors,* a delectable homage to the low-budget horror films of the fifties. It succeeded because they knew the secret of satire: playing it absolutely straight. It got overblown into an apocalyptic vision when it was filmed, of course, with all the subtlety of a cattle prod. The duo next wrote songs for Disney. Their first original film, the last that Ashman lived to see, was *The Little Mermaid.* Then came *Beauty and the Beast.* Ashman would be astonished to know of his continuing success, in these three years following his death. Why, even this year, he had a new show open on Broadway: *Beauty and the Beast.* Amazing what Disney muscle and money can do.

S ober, Conrad Veidt was straight. But drunk? Watch your goodies, boys. In his American movies he specialized in playing cruel, ice-cold Nazis. ("Ve haff vays of making you talk...") The facts were quite contradictory. A great star in his native Germany *(The Cabinet of Dr Caligari, Richard III, The Hands of Orlac),* he became internationally famous with *The Student of Prague.* Hollywood pounced. The advent of sound took him back to Germany but having a Jewish wife soon made escape to England imperative. A chance return to Germany resulted in the Nazis detaining the couple. When his British employers rescued them with *much* difficulty, he gratefully became a British citizen. In 1940, he returned to Hollywood, capping a great career by playing the poisonous Major Strasser in *Casablanca.*

aulette Goddard never had the career she deserved, and she missed landing the part of Scarlett O'Hara by a *squeak*. Too bad, for she was a truly enchanting minx, with an adroit gift for comedy. She started out playing bits, and caught the eye of Charlie Chaplin. He was bewitched by her crisp beauty and tart wit, and secretly married her. Her first plum role was the adorable guttersnipe in his *Modern Times*. Some of her other films were classics, too: *The Women, The Great Dictator, Anna Lucasta, Reap the Wild Wind,* but her career stopped short in the fifties. Three other husbands followed Chaplin, but, really, marriage was merely a convenience. She died wealthy, but spent her capital lavishly on young artists, a *prodigiously* generous patron of the arts.

The great eccentric actor Ernest Thesiger first flickered onto a screen in 1918, and didn't flicker off it until 1961, supporting Warren Beatty in *The Roman Spring of Mrs. Stone*. Thesiger was a languid skeleton, a wisp of smoke made flesh. Some actors sweat blood for their art, some disappear into their roles; Thesiger could get away with performances composed almost entirely of filigree. Watch him perform the part of the ethereal imp Dr. Praetorius in *The Bride of Frankenstein*. He handles that cigar as if it were a dildo he might just transmogrify into a butterfly. Even seated quietly off the set he was unique, working away at an ever-present piece of embroidery, a mad amalgam of black widow spider and Don Knotts. *Exquisite.*

No, Jesus Christ was neither gay nor a member of the film colony. (As far as I know...) The gentleman above is simply doing an impression of Him. He is H.B. Warner, who originally played Our Lord in Cecil B. DeMille's silent version of *King of Kings*. Warner was the son of British stage actor Charles Warner, and after a false start in medicine, he followed in his father's footsteps. He began film work in 1914, carving out a long and moderately glorious movie career. (It should be mentioned that he generally played somewhat more earthbound parts than the above.) All of us are familiar with one of his later characters, the drunken druggist in that perennial Christmas classic, *It's a Wonderful Life*. And it was.

You have a choice, dear boy," warned Laurence Olivier. "You can be one of the greatest actors of our time, or you can become a household word." Richard Burton took the easier route, opting to wallow in millions of lovely dollars, adulation by multitudes, day-and-night media coverage, and the ample charms of the luxurious Liz. Not a bad deal, you might say, but a price was exacted. The scripts got worse, the good work faded from memory, and a stupendously gifted actor turned into a bad joke. His catalog of hackwork is painful to relate: *The Klansman, Trotsky, Exorcist II* ... need I go on? Well, perhaps his judgment was clouded by booze. Burton claimed to have tried men in his green and adventurous youth, "but it didn't work."

Rudy Vallee, saxophonist and bandleader, was the first pop singer to be termed a crooner. Clutching his trademark megaphone, he was cornier than most, but *catnip* to female fans. When smoother singers like Bing Crosby stole his fire, he segued into movies as a fine character actor, screamingly funny in pictures like Preston Sturges's *The Palm Beach Story*. He wasn't averse to poking a little fun at his own image either. But later in life he became something of a pest to the city fathers in Los Angeles by his tiresome petitions to have the street he lived on changed to Rue de Vallee. And even later, anyone who heard him cringed at his senile bragging that he had bedded thousands of women. Especially anyone familiar with his *real* sexual history.

Oh, Dearest Diary,
   Golly-goshums, life is grim! Oh, where to start? First, the plastic surgeons tell me I've run out of features to alter! And I've had to pay *oodles* of money, 'cause one of the guys' mommies has accused me of *unspeakable* acts — honest, we were just playing *doctor* ... (oh, *dear*, those policemen had cold hands!) ... LaToya — *my own sister* — keeps saying wicked things about me in public! Those mean old tabloids are trying to say I'm GAY, and I'm not, I'm not, I'm *not!* Gee, maybe I should get married. Now, let's see ... Princess Di's not free yet ... the Virgin Mary's out ... oh, dear diary, where's the one for me?

   Till tomorrow,
   Michael

Cole Porter wedded graceful tunes to witty, elegantly smutty lyrics. But he must have been disappointed by what Hollywood did to some of his scores. *The Gay Divorcée*, for instance, was gutted of all but one of its songs, "Night and Day." *Panama Hattie, Let's Face It, DuBarry Was a Lady* — all suffered similar indignities. So Porter simply composed scores directly for Hollywood. A wealthy playboy and *bon vivant*, he worked hard, and suffered, too. While riding a horse one day, he was thrown; his mount rolled over on him, crushing his legs. Porter blithely claimed to have worked on the lyric for "At Long Last Love" while waiting for help, but the accident resulted in years of agony, dozens of operations over the years, and an eventual amputation.

It must have galled George Cukor to be called "a woman's director" (Hollywood shorthand for "faggot") with such regularity. It neatly put him in his place: a nice little director who could handle the ladies. His gayness gave Clark Gable the muscle to get him fired from *Gone with the Wind* too, even if the *real* reason was Gable's hysterical fear that with Cukor directing, Vivien Leigh would upstage him. But even hardened homophobes had to admit he had one of the best batting averages in film history. And he directed men with sensitivity, too. While rehearsing Jack Lemmon for his first movie, he kept saying to the actor, "Less, less!" Lemmon finally sputtered, "Soon I won't be acting at all!" Cukor smiled and said, *"Now* you're getting the idea."

A sadistic, alcoholic slattern, a determined southern belle; an avaricious waitress, a Bronx housewife determined to give her daughter a proper wedding; a tart Welsh schoolteacher; a homicidal adulteress; floozies, pathetic old maids, scheming wives, career women, or England's greatest queen: there was no part Bette Davis couldn't tackle. The role of wife and mother she found more of a stretch, as her loathsome daughter B.D. pointed out in an vengeful, exploitative book. It didn't matter much. What counted was that glorious body of work, which nobody will probably ever match. Above, in *All about Eve,* she played the role that revived a fading career: a Broadway star feeling age's winged chariot hurrying near. And she was the *greatest* of gay icons.

Roger Edens began by arranging special material for Ethel Merman at Paramount. His next job, as MGM musical supervisor, introduced him to a fresh young talent whose career he was to influence profoundly, Judy Garland. Nobody did more to shape her film persona, to guide her through the Hollywood thickets, and it was back-breaking work. But he hung on, dispensing advice, sometimes only providing a shoulder to cry on. But nothing could break her dying fall. His own career included producing and even songwriting (his additional material for *Funny Face* nicely complemented the Gershwins' work). He ended up on Broadway, training Katharine Hepburn to sing her way through the musical *Coco.* Poor man. Not even dedication, hard work, or prayer can accomplish everything; she *still* sounded like Donald Duck.

Throughout the fifties and sixties, whenever a television sitcom script required a fussbudget, a stuffy father, a busybody neighbor, they called on one of the finest character actors of TV's golden age: Richard Deacon. He was superb comic relief on many a show, but the best role to fall into his capable hands was the much-put-upon bald producer Mel Cooley, in the late, great *Dick Van Dyke Show*. There, he found a perfect foil in Morey Amsterdam. Their confrontations, with Mel usually sent spluttering from the room, were truly great shtick. When acting finally became a chore, the ebullient gay actor turned to writing cookbooks. And he did showbiz a final favor when he discovered and nurtured the talent of cafe singer Michael Feinstein.

100

Cavernous dimples, soft caterpillar eyebrows, vaguely British accent — Peter Lawford was a light, *very* light leading man in MGM comedies and musicals of the late forties. After the first blush of youth, roles diminished — in the way such roles will. So he segued into television, with middling success *(The Thin Man)*. But his greatest fame came as Jack Kennedy's brother-in-law and member of Frank Sinatra's "Rat Pack." He kept working but, hey, pimping for the Kennedy boys was *far* easier work than acting. More fun, too. Some even say that it was Lawford who tucked the fair Marilyn between JFK's sheets. When his marriage to Pat Kennedy ended, he married again, but he was gay nonetheless. His mother, the witty and outspoken Lady Lawford, certainly said so, *often*.

Tom Hulce is one of only a handful of openly gay actors. Debuting in James Bridges's sentimental *September 30, 1955*, his first big hit was that carnival of gross-out humor, *National Lampoon's Animal House*, a movie noteworthy for introducing a whole slew of up-and-coming actors. Hulce's unhandsome, lived-in face is a terrific asset, assuring his casting in an array of splendid character parts: the braying, childish Mozart in *Amadeus*, the borderline retarded trashman Dominick, in *Dominick and Eugene*, and perhaps best of all, the scapegrace younger brother undeserving of his father's devotion in *Parenthood*. Hulce has also done some remarkable stage work as well, notably, in the London production of Larry Kramer's *The Normal Heart*. Here's a career to watch.

Drag, swear its practitioners on a stack of *Vogue* magazines, is very liberating. If they're right, female impersonator Craig Russell soared like an eagle. In street clothes, the Canadian actor was a mere face in the crowd. But when caught in that intoxicating beam of pink and amber, the wren became a bird of paradise. Russell only displayed his impressions of Garland, Mae West, and Bette Davis in a couple of movies, but luckily *Outrageous!* was one of them. It's a sweet little drama about a drab hairdresser who moonlights in organdy and ostrich plumes, and who suddenly finds himself playing mother hen to a young pregnant mental patient. Mere flamboyance is not enough to carry off such a part, what's required is a vulnerable humanity. Russell had it in abundance.

Tony Richardson's first professional venue was London's Royal Court Theatre, directing the original production of John Osborne's *Look Back in Anger*, among many others. He brought it to the screen three years later, the first of a string of visually inventive films like *A Taste of Honey*, *The Loneliness of the Long Distance Runner*, and Olivier's great triumph, *The Entertainer*. Fine movies, of course. But his masterpiece was *Tom Jones*, a rowdy roller-coaster ride of randiness, a movie he could never top. (His graveyard satire *The Loved One* appears almost tame today — apart from the jaw-dropping, eye-popping sight of the gluttonous Mrs. Joyboy.) Although Richardson was married to Vanessa Redgrave for a time, not even that enchantress could keep him away from the butterfly boys of Soho.

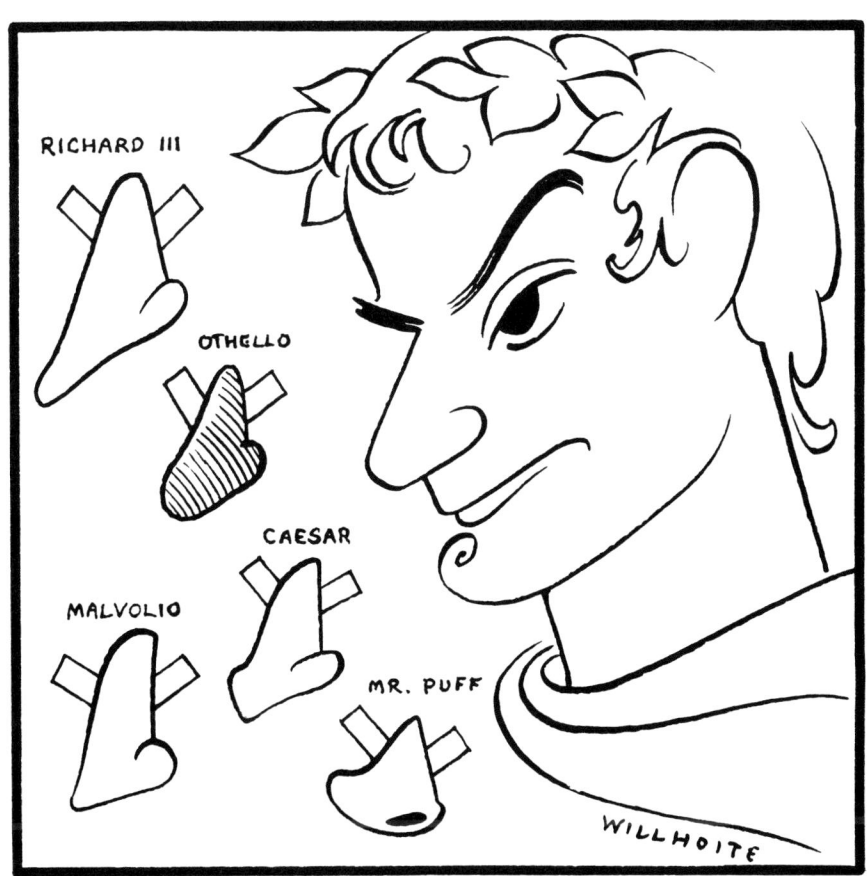

Laurence Olivier, that most physical of actors, was by common consent the greatest actor of the century. Because he employed makeup so extensively, it was said that he never played a part in his own nose. But his protean quality really came from the inside. He could act any role, it seemed; in *Othello* alone he ran the gamut from Uncle Tom to Little Eva. Olivier seemed cozily at home in any of Shakespeare's heroic roles, but he claimed that his favorite (and most personal) part was the cheap music-hall hack Archie Rice, in *The Entertainer*. Olivier was not, strictly speaking, gay, but in his memoirs (a notoriously reticent book) he admitted to youthful experimentation. Only after his death did word of his affair with Danny Kaye appear in print.

While the top male stars were off fighting World War II, Van Johnson, former Broadway chorus boy, neatly stepped in and became a top box-office draw. He was the boy next door, freckles, white teeth — the whole package. And the female public responded by sending him masses of homemade cookies. A song-and-dance man and deft light comedian, he later attempted to shake his boyish image by springing a few dramatic roles on the public *(The Caine Mutiny,* for example). Best friend to Keenan Wynn, he ran off with Wynn's wife, only to leave her, she said, for a male dancer. His career had fizzled out by the 1970s, but he magically appeared in Woody Allen's *The Purple Rose of Cairo,* a bit stout, but charm quite undiminished.

Death can do *wonders* for a career. Take Marilyn Monroe. Almost immediately, her mysterious demise resulted in a flood of books, plays, and movies which shows no sign of abating. Why? Well, her appeal may lie in her complexity, for she was a tumult of contradictions. The childlike love goddess was a vulnerable product of child abuse, illegitimate, unwanted, passed around. The instinctive, sparkling comedienne was an unreliable monster who in her neurotic last years would barely condescend to visit the set. An unattainable angel, she was also a sex toy ruthlessly exploited by agents, producers, and other Hollywood vermin — and even by a president. And although almost frighteningly heterosexual, she was available to *anyone* who was willing to comfort her. Even, for a while, to a female drama coach.

Perhaps it's a shame that Jim Nabors is so closely identified in the public's mind as the cornpone TV character Gomer Pyle. He might have been *Mrs.* Rock Hudson! Back in the midseventies, when hardly anyone in Hollywood seemed to be out of the closet, these two were rumored to have gotten married. Nobody seems to know precisely what happened, but it seems that a practical joke must have gotten out of hand. The fallout was embarrassing for everyone, though Rock Hudson, being a much bigger star, weathered it better. But Gomer's burgeoning career as a nightclub singer was somewhat crippled. (His rather too rich and plummy baritone was a little alarming anyway.) But his recordings sold well enough — back on television ... *Heeere's* how to *order!*

Oliver Stone has approached moviemaking from the back door. This child of privilege arrived in Vietnam to teach English in 1965, just as the war was heating up in earnest. From there, as a merchant seaman, he sailed to Guadalajara, and settled down to write a huge shapeless novel, *A Child's Night Dream.* It turned out *not* to be his passport to fame. That would come much later. The great war movie *Platoon* made him into an "overnight" success, and such movies as *Wall Street* and *JFK* have made him one of the town's high rollers. Pressured by an *Advocate* interview, the happily married Stone admitted readily that, yes, he has had sex with men. (He didn't go into any details, so we'll have to be satisfied with that.)

Most couch potatoes don't know of Michael Jeter as the star of a Broadway musical, but that's how he made his first big breakthrough, after years of struggle. In the darkly romantic *Grand Hotel* he played the most endearing of the many characters, the dying bookkeeper who suddenly takes center stage with his wild Charleston, "Who Couldn't Dance with You?" Indeed, his real forte may just be the *completely* unexpected specialty turn. In *The Fisher King*, that blackest of black comedies, he is a comic miracle doing a drag act atop a desk, singing "Let Me Entertain You" with all the abandon of a hopped-up Liza Minnelli. TV has discovered him too, and although he fits in nicely with the ensemble of *Evening Shade*, he could probably carry it alone.

Okay, so the world has one less doctor. When Lily Tomlin gave up her premed studies at Wayne State to go into comedy full-time, the world should have given a huge collective sigh of relief. In 1966, she began playing New York's comedy clubs, did a few commercials, and finally hit the big time, television's *The Garry Moore Show*. Her lavish, chaotic gifts of characterization came to full bloom a couple of years later, on *Rowan and Martin's Laugh-In*. Movies were inevitable, even if an early try was *Moment by Moment*, a classic stinker. Since that time, she has become more actress than comic; and maybe she always was. But she can still drive audiences into frenzied laughter, with material by her equally gifted life-partner Jane Wagner.

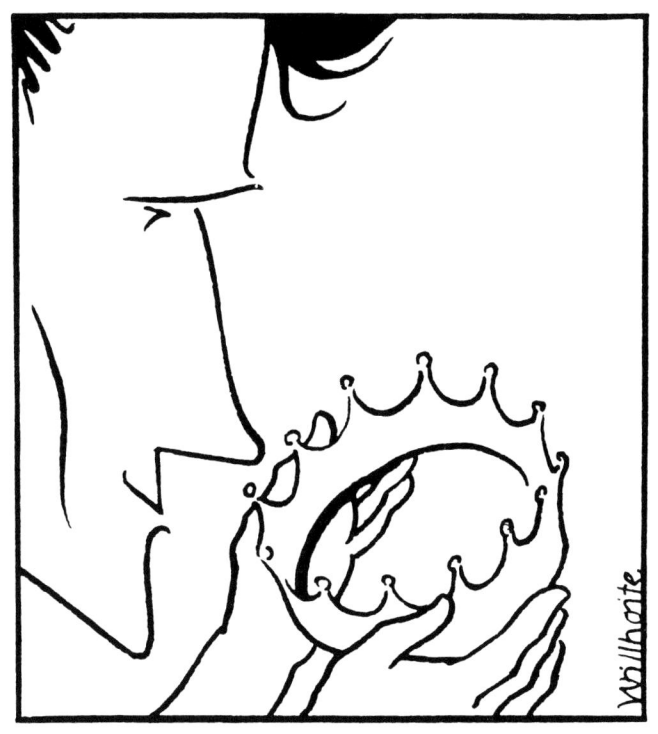

Lithuania's gift to the screen, Lauruska Mischa Skikne, became famous as Laurence Harvey. Enrolling in Britain's Royal Academy of Dramatic Art, he developed into a fine Shakespearean actor, and debuted onscreen in 1948. Harvey was always a curiously detached actor. Simone Signoret found him so withdrawn in their love scenes in *Room at the Top* that she later declared that dialogue with him was like reading alone. Love scenes weren't really his thing. (The reason isn't difficult to fathom.) When given the role of Raymond Shaw in *The Manchurian Candidate*, he must have been relieved to finally play a man as dégagé as his own rather frosty self. In that splendid satirical thriller, Harvey is beautifully cast. He seems always on the verge of breaking through his isolation. And always failing.

Flaming youth! Bathtub gin! William Haines was the breeziest sheik in the silent college comedies. He was good enough to pull off dramatic roles too, but to his adoring public, he was forever fixed in amber as a male flapper. (His box-office clout, according to Hollywood legend, enabled him to engage the young, ambitious Clark Gable to service him once.) Haines was determined to have fun *off*-camera too and MGM had to quash *scads* of newspaper stories, none involving girls. Eventually the studio pressured Haines into announcing a marriage to Pola Negri. That called off the newshounds temporarily, but nothing lasts forever, and many-tongued rumor ultimately forced Haines to retire. With his lover and former stand-in, Jimmy Shields, he became a top Hollywood interior decorator.

113

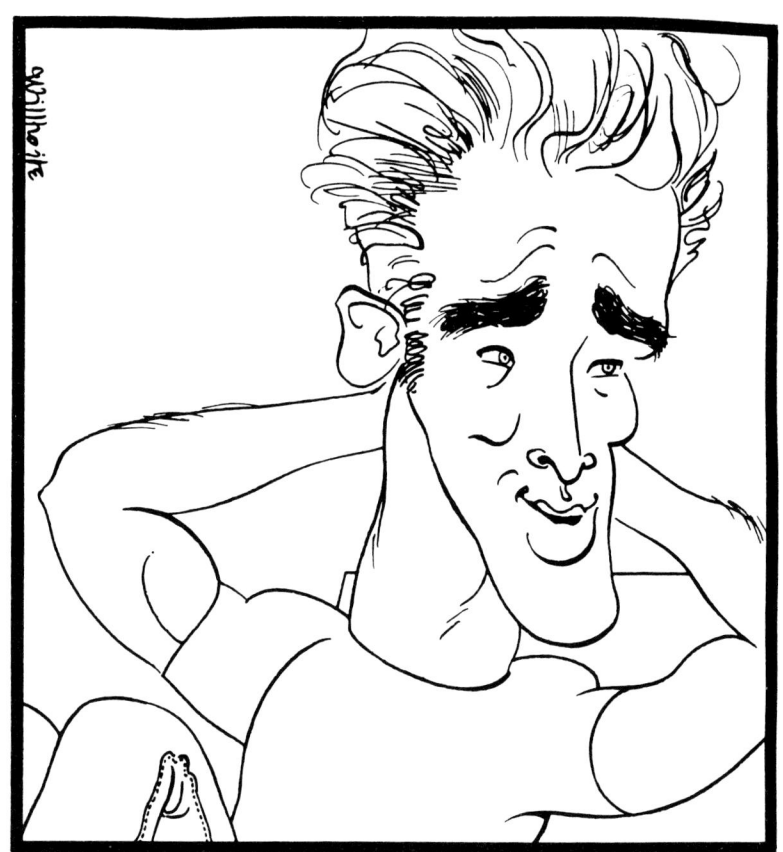

To this day, there are people who hotly deny that James Dean was gay. (Just as there are probably people who claim to play bridge every Tuesday with Marie Antoinette, Hitler, and Proust.) What nobody can persuasively deny is the fact of Dean's genius. Watch *East of Eden.* If you don't believe you've just seen what acting is all about, rewind the tape and watch it again — carefully. We may never again see an actor with such native gifts. (All right, Leonardo DiCaprio comes close.) Dean only starred in three movies, *Eden, Giant,* and *Rebel without a Cause,* so when he and his Porsche ended up smeared all over the highway, he easily passed into the realm of legend. He never got the chance to fail.

In the thirties Charles Walters was a featured juvenile in a couple of Cole Porter musicals, not a bad start. Dimpled, dark-lashed, and athletic, Walters was handsome enough to coast on his looks, but choreography, he knew, would take him further. In the early forties MGM beckoned. The dancing he created for such classics as *Meet Me in St. Louis* indicated to the studio that Walters could direct. (After all, Vincente Minnelli couldn't handle *everything*.) So it fell to Walters to direct gems like *Easter Parade, The Barkleys of Broadway, Lili, High Society,* and other musicals and light comedies. He even returned as a performer in one film, guiding the formidable Joan Crawford around the dance floor in *Torch Song,* the high noon of her suffering-in-mink period. Brave man!

Scorsese's *The King of Comedy* introduced many to Sandra Bernhard for the first time. This scabrous gender-bender comic can be poignant, funny, and in-your-face in rapid succession. Lips flying in every direction, intense aquiline eyes boring into the audience's, she might make you acutely uncomfortable — but try *not* to laugh. For a while a self-confessed bisexual, she changed her mind a bit later. Anyway, the bulletin changes pretty well weekly. (Interspecies relationships are not outside the realm of possibility...) Her "affair" with Madonna, if it really was that, seemed more an attempt to shock than to get down and have a bit of fun. But it takes superhuman energy to compete with Madonna in the *épater le bourgeois* department, so Bernhard moved on. Stay tuned.

Nazi spy, child molester, homosexual, Howard Hughes's boyfriend ... They've tried to pin a *lot* of things on Errol Flynn. (Well, the last two charges could be made to stick.) An early film, *Captain Blood,* led to a colorful series of costume swashbucklers. But his career played second fiddle to a rapacious libido. Some wear their hearts on their sleeves; Flynn wore his pecker. And what the hell, who *wouldn't* succumb to his spell? He was a sexy animal, athletic, gorgeous, a hedonist's hedonist. Boys, girls, three wives, a sailboat he unabashedly adored — movies played a subordinate role to pleasure. In his last three roles he played drunks, but by then role and actor had fused. He was fifty when he died, but the coroner cut up a *much* older man.

Let's shower together! Anthony Perkins was bopping along as a gangling, girl-shy teenage type when Alfred Hitchcock signed him to play Norman Bates in the pioneer shocker *Psycho*. It was a stroke of casting genius. Something in Perkins's soft, boyish winsomeness made the frenzied attack that much more jolting when it burst through the shower curtains at Janet Leigh. He was a consistently busy film actor, admittedly in rather offbeat parts. He even tried a Broadway musical, *Greenwillow*, and he wasn't half-bad. But later the easy dough of cheesy *Psycho* "sequels" was too tempting to refuse. In another sense he was *always* Norman Bates, very uncertain about his sexuality, fighting his gayness, and *trying* not to be cruel to his army of ex-lovers but never quite succeeding...

Nick Adams's specialty was playing disaffected youth, but he didn't mind dropping the scowl for a while to play comedy, like *No Time for Sergeants,* above. The diminutive actor was, as the times seemed to call for, a maverick (that Brando influence *again*). So naturally, his hit TV series was called *The Rebel.* A roomie to James Dean, Adams was (oh, *lucky* man!) probably for a time his lover. Not a bad fantasy, anyway. At his death he was alleged to be something more than a friend to a noted hunk later known for his work in various miniseries. Adams died of an overdose, like many a young firebrand, but it seems to have been tied to a nervous disorder he was being treated for, not recreation.

Television is a capricious medium. Even more than movies or theatre, it rapidly takes up performers and then discards them, and today's star may be tomorrow's pizza waitress. Judy Carne, a charming gamine, never really made it big. She first got caught up in a couple of moderately entertaining sitcoms, *The Baileys of Balboa* and *Love on a Rooftop*. They were gone in a twinkling but she had better luck on her next outing, as the sock-it-to-me girl on *Rowan and Martin's Laugh-In*. The poor kid took more water in the face than Greg Louganis, but what the hell, she was a name for a few seasons. Nothing else seemed to work out as well afterwards, especially her strangest role: the first Mrs. Burt Reynolds.

Dick Sargent wasn't TV's luckiest sitcomic. On the short-lived *Broadside* he was billed *waaaay* down the line in a cast of women. In *Down to Earth,* he played opposite three adorable moppets, a disadvantageous position at best. Worst of all was the *Tammy Grimes Show,* in which he played her twin brother Terrence, which was stretching it *just* a bit. (Sargent was sort of cute; Grimes, however a major talent, had the face of Charlie Chaplin's left shoe.) His biggest break, alas, was playing second banana to Elizabeth Montgomery's twitching nose in *Bewitched.* A replacement, at that, for departing Dick York. Sargent deserved better. He was more attractive than York (no contest — Chaplin's *right* shoe) *and* gay, as he blithely confided to millions of viewers a few years ago.

A commission from the Asia Society first took director James Ivory to India to make a documentary. There he acquired two great partners, producer Ismail Merchant and screenwriter Ruth Prawer Jhabvala. This inspired trio began with a tricky form, the serious comedy of manners, and mastered it in films like *Shakespeare Wallah*. They ventured into *very* strange waters with *The Wild Party*, but in *The Europeans* everything came back into focus. Ivory's great films *Howard's End* and *The Remains of the Day* have endured a lot of flak from obtuse critics implying that literature and film don't belong together. A celestial comedy like *A Room with a View* makes such carping laughable. He may direct greater movies in future, but there will *never* be a sunnier romance put to film than this Anglo-Italian idyll. His charming, ebullient partner Ismail Merchant (shown opposite) recently joined the fraternity of directors too, with the graceful film *In Custody*. And in two of his cookbooks, *Indian Cuisine* and *Passionate Meals,* this hearty amateur chef has shared his love of Indian food with the rest of us.

Liam Neeson isn't Northern Ireland's only gift to the movies. Max Adrian was a grandiloquent actor of the old school who knew *exactly* at which point to stop chewing the scenery: when it had been reduced to pulp. His natural province was the stage, where he created the role of Dr. Pangloss in Leonard Bernstein's brilliant *Candide.* He also toured in the one-man show *By George,* impersonating George Bernard Shaw. His film work was sporadic but flavorful. Late in life he was discovered by the equally colorful Ken Russell and cast in three of his movies. In *The Music Lovers,* he was the composer Rubinstein; in *The Boy Friend,* the exquisitely hammy impresario. But in *The Devils,* his baroque excesses came across as almost *normal.*

itchell Leisen designed costumes for DeMille in the silent era. But by the thirties Leisen himself was a top director, bringing his highly visual style to a wide variety of films. This "woman's director" was especially adept at guiding his leading ladies through comedy. Colbert in *Midnight;* Stanwyck in *Remember the Night;* and best of all, Jean Arthur in the sublime screwball farce *Easy Living.* Leisen, the compleat filmmaker, acted in *Hold Back the Dawn,* produced several of his other films, and always managed to keep his hand in costume design. But when his touch turned to lead in his later films, he tried television (finesse being dispensable to *The Lucy Show).* By that time, interior decoration (with his lover, Billy Daniels) was his main focus anyway.

British novelist Hanif Kureishi has always had one foot in the hurly-burly of showbiz, it seems. While writing, he worked at least part-time in the theatre, odd jobs like stage managing, box-office clerking, and even moving scenery. But we celebrate him for his witty, gritty screenplays for *My Beautiful Laundrette* and *Sammy and Rosie Get Laid*. The former was one of the earliest exposures American audiences had to the gifted young actor Daniel Day-Lewis, giving a wonderfully unselfconscious performance as the street rowdy in love with a young Pakistani man. Kureishi, who is prolific enough as a novelist, obviously believes in keeping fluid by working in film, too. *And* he has also written for Thames Television.

One of the wittiest, best-written sitcoms of the sixties was *The Many Loves of Dobie Gillis*. Poor dumb Dobie: he wanted a *goddess,* and all he could get was Zelda Gilroy. The sap didn't know how lucky he was. Zelda was played by ponytailed Sheila James, a perky pixie who projected intelligence as well as adorability. When the program ended, she tried another show, *Broadside,* which folded in a wink. James was bright enough to take that as a sign, that *and* being targeted as lesbian. So she enrolled in Harvard Law, founded the California Women's Law Center, and made a name for herself (her *real* one, Sheila Kuehl) as a crusader for all the right causes. She's terrific, she's necessary, and damned if she isn't *still* adorable.

Although Robert Morse's province is the musical theatre, his dozen or so movies make one long for more. Nobody else could have played Pierpont Finch in *How to Succeed in Business without Really Trying*. And in *The Loved One*, his outlandish presence was the only logical casting. The man is, it must be admitted, ugly as a mud turtle, but strangely cute at the same time, which he was best able to turn to advantage when he played Truman Capote in a highly successful one-man show, *Tru*. This dedicated father of three once casually told an interviewer for *The Advocate* that he was bisexual. But in the musical *Sugar*, he was so achingly funny in drag that it's easy to imagine he's not a bad mom, either.

If pressed to name several Hollywood costume designers, most people could come up with only one name: Edith Head. She was a teacher at first, but film's siren song called her, and by the late 1930s she was the head designer at Paramount. Many of Hollywood's leading ladies swore by her, and even made her employment on their pictures a contractual necessity. Elizabeth Taylor, Audrey Hepburn, Bette Davis, Olivia de Havilland, Jennifer Jones, a whole *slew* of star actresses thought that Head was the best in the business. They must have been right: eight Oscars, folks. *Eight*. A modest little wren of a woman, she was one of our own but kept her personal life very much to herself.

In Bertolucci's groundbreaking *Last Tango in Paris*, Maria Schneider was a yummy little love-muffin, rolling about in the buff with Marlon Brando. (Incidentally, why did *he* remain mostly clothed...?) It was as popular as pizza all over the world, but it also got the director and his two stars in rather a pretty pickle in Italy: they were indicted for obscenity for making the film. (I know: *Italians* upset about the *erotic?*) Schneider, the daughter of French superstar Daniel Gelin, enjoyed a modest career after *Tango*, although aside from her role opposite Jack Nicholson in *The Passenger*, she never achieved great popularity in America. It's tempting to speculate whether her lack of favor over here was tied in with her breezy announcement in the midseventies that she was bisexual.

Oh, those great Hollywood names! Rock, Dack, Rip, Tab. *Ahhh,* Tab Hunter, one of the great masturbatory fantasy figures of the fifties! To characterize him as a, well, *sensitive* Aldo Ray would diminish him somewhat, but it's not far off the mark, either. Tab was groomed to be another milk-and-cookies Boy Next Door, so his movie roles were lightweight to a fault. But so was he. He never got a role that really challenged him, but got things just right in the musical *Damn Yankees.* A nice little career, yes, but it faltered badly when a story hit the papers in which he was accused of viciously beating his dog. He lay fallow for a few years, then — surprise! — rose like a phoenix with a new leading lady — *Divine!*

When most people think of Charles Nelson Reilly, they think of the flamboyant, bespectacled twit featured on such TV game shows as *Hollywood Squares*; in other words, your generic TV "personality." Many don't realize that he first made his reputation as a solid character actor in musical theatre, and has been cited (correctly) as having the perfect musical comedy voice. He first made his name as the boss's nephew, Bud Frump, attempting to thwart Robert Morse at every turn in *How to Succeed in Business without Really Trying*. In *Skyscraper*, he was foil to Julie Harris in her sole musical comedy outing. And in *Hello, Dolly!* he even played the romantic lead. But the easy bucks of television are seductive, and the medium seems to suit him.

With legs an ostrich would *die* for and a smile that could melt the polar ice cap, Tommy Tune is the type of talent that lopes into view too seldom. And yes, it's his real name. His film debut was in *Hello, Dolly*, in which he was spectacularly wasted. (Nobody was allowed to look at anyone but Barbra Streisand — *she* saw to that.) Two years later, he appeared, again to little effect, in Ken Russell's grotesque take on *The Boy Friend*. Two negligible credits. So the Texas tornado blew onto a grateful Broadway. As a director-choreographer *(Grand Hotel, Nine, Will Rogers Follies)* this genial genius is the great hope of the musical theatre. And on those too-rare occasions when he performs, *run*, don't walk for tickets.

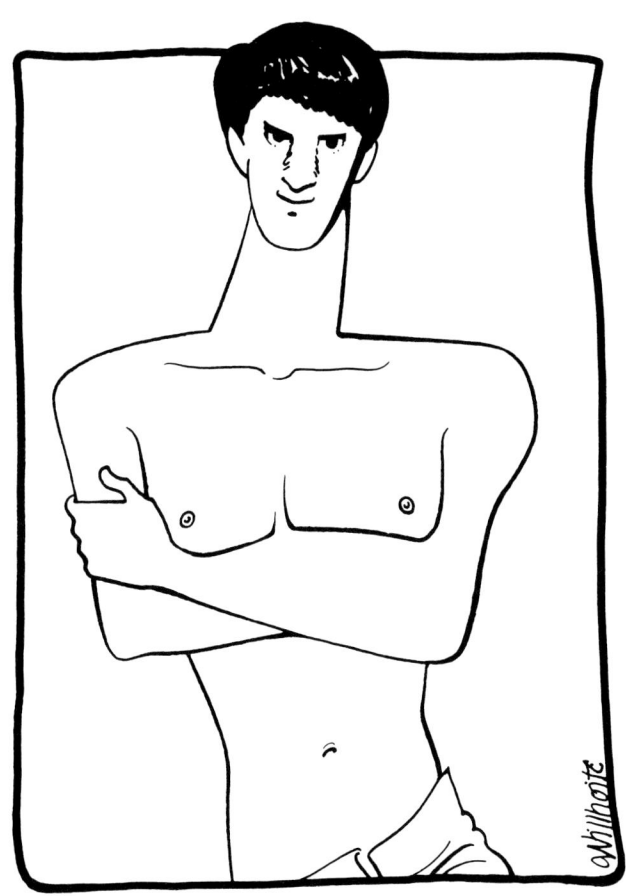

Okay. How do you parlay a talent no bigger than a hamster's clitoris into stardom? Well, if you're Madonna, a genius for publicity can pretty well do the trick. If you're Casey Donovan — bare those buns, baby! A former schoolteacher, Calvin Culver longed to get into showbiz. He first tried the stage, and when that didn't work out, he found his career was more likely to take off if he, well, took it *all* off. Porn requires zilch talent beyond a certain, er, rigidity, and one hardly requires a name to put into the credits. But Donovan's drop-dead beauty and phenomenal physique caused fans to clamor for his identity. I mean, when you manage to launch a million wet dreams, you *deserve* a moniker.

Carole Landis was a star, all right. But she twinkled dimly and too briefly, barely a decade. Her celebrity brightened the war years. She churned out multiple movies, mostly musicals, *six* in 1941 alone. Occasionally, she landed a winner like *Topper Returns* or *I Wake Up Screaming,* but generally they were routine affairs like *Four Jills in a Jeep,* based on her experiences entertaining Our Brave Boys. Landis deserved better; she had real talent, great legs, and a way with a song. But nobody could assuage her cosmic loneliness, not the four husbands, the numerous affairs (including one with the young Jacqueline Susann before her trashy novel days), and certainly not the married Rex Harrison. So she finally sought oblivion in a handful of sleeping pills.

INDEX

Adams, Nick, 119
Adrian, Max, 124
Arzner, Dorothy, 31
Ashman, Howard, 88
Beaton, Cecil, 20
Bernhard, Sandra, 116
Brando, Marlon, 63
Bridges, James, 15
Brooks, Louise, 60
Buchanan, Jack, 65
Burr, Raymond, 19
Burton, Richard, 93
Callow, Simon, 46
Carne, Judy, 120
Cassidy, David, 66
Cassidy, Jack, 86
Charleson, Ian, 47
Clift, Montgomery, 29
Crawford, Joan, 14
Cukor, George, 97
Dailey, Dan, 56
Davis, Bette, 98
De Wolfe, Billy, 32
Deacon, Richard, 100
Dean, James, 114
Dekker, Albert, 59
Del Rio, Dolores, 54
Dietrich, Marlene, 18
Divine, 33
Donovan, Casey, 134
Eddy, Nelson, 67
Edens, Roger, 99
Fierstein, Harvey, 37
Flowers, Wayland, 53
Flynn, Errol, 117
Frey, Leonard, 87
Gable, Clark, 78
Garbo, Greta, 76
Garfield, John, 42
Garland, Judy, 73
Gaynor, Janet, 44
Geer, Will, 36

Geffen, David, 17
Gibbons, Cedric, 55
Gielgud, John, 23
Goddard, Paulette, 90
Goulding, Edmund, 51
Grant, Cary, 82
Haines, William, 113
Harvey, Laurence, 112
Head, Edith, 129
Higgins, Colin, 84
Holliday, Judy, 64
Horton, Edward Everett, 81
Hudson, Rock, 35
Hughes, Howard, 48
Hulce, Tom, 102
Hunter, Tab, 131
Ivory, James, 122
Jackson, Michael, 95
James Kuehl, Sheila, 127
Jeter, Michael, 110
Johnson, Van, 106
Kaye, Danny, 70
Kirk, Tommy, 16
Kureishi, Hanif, 126
La Rocque, Rod, 61
Landis, Carole, 135
Laughton, Charles, 80
Lawford, Peter, 101
Lawrence, Gertrude, 25
Leisen, Mitchell, 125
Lillie, Beatrice, 57
Lorre, Peter, 10
Lynde, Paul, 40
McDaniel, Hattie, 21
Merchant, Ismail, 123
Mineo, Sal, 26
Minnelli, Liza, 74
Minnelli, Vincente, 72
Monroe, Marilyn, 107
Moorehead, Agnes, 49
Morse, Robert, 128
Murnau, F.W., 41

Nabors, Jim, 108
Nader, George, 71
Nazimova, Alla, 38
Nelson, Ricky, 22
Novarro, Ramon, 58
Olivier, Laurence, 105
Pangborn, Franklin, 43
Perkins, Anthony, 118
Porter, Cole, 96
Power, Tyrone, 27
Rambova, Natasha, 69
Redgrave, Michael, 30
Reilly, Charles Nelson, 132
Richardson, Tony, 104
Romero, Cesar, 11
Russell, Craig, 103
Sargent, Dick, 121
Schlesinger, John, 45
Schneider, Maria, 130
Scott, Randolph, 83
Stanwyck, Barbara, 12
Stiller, Mauritz, 77
Stone, Oliver, 109
Taylor, Robert, 13
Taylor, William Desmond, 75
Thesiger, Ernest, 91
Thompson, Kay, 52
Tomlin, Lily, 111
Tune, Tommy, 133
Valentino, Rudolph, 68
Vallee, Rudy, 94
Veidt, Conrad, 89
Visconti, Luchino, 39
Walters, Charles, 115
Warner, H.B., 92
Waters, Ethel, 85
Waters, John, 24
Webb, Clifton, 28
Whale, James, 50
Williams, Emlyn, 34
Woolley, Monty, 79
Zeffirelli, Franco, 62